The
1968 Nortl
Bus Hand.

British Bus Publishing

Body codes used in the heritage Bus Handbook series:

Type:

A	Articulated vehicle
B	Single-deck bus
C	Coach - High-back seating
D	Low floor double-deck bus (4-metre)
DP	Express - high-back seating in a bus body
H	Full-height double-deck
L	Low-height double-deck
M	Minibus
N	Low-floor bus
O	Open-top bus (CO = convertible)
P	Partial or convertible open-top

Seating capacity is then shown. For double-decks the upper deck first,

Door position:-

C	Centre entrance/exit
D	Dual doorway
F	Front entrance/exit
R	Rear entrance/exit
T	Three or more access points

Equipment:-

L	Lift for wheelchair
T	Toilet

e.g. - H32/28F is a high-bridge bus with thirty-two seats upstairs, twenty-eight down and a front entrance/exit.
B43D is a bus with two doorways.

Books in the regional series:

The Scottish Bus Handbook
The Ireland & Islands Bus Handbook
The North East Bus Handbook
The Yorkshire Bus Handbook
The Lancashire, Cumbria and Manchester Bus Handbook
The Merseyside and Cheshire Bus Handbook
The North and West Midlands Bus Handbook
The East Midlands Bus Handbook
The South Midlands Bus Handbook
The North and West Wales Bus Handbook
The South Wales Bus Handbook
The Chilterns & West Anglia Bus Handbook
The East Anglia Bus Handbook
The South West Bus Handbook
The South Central Bus Handbook
The South East Bus Handbook

Annual books are produced for the major groups:

The Stagecoach Bus Handbook
The FirstBus Bus Handbook
The Arriva Bus Handbook

Associated series:

The Hong Kong Bus Handbook
The Leyland Lynx Handbook
The Model Bus Handbook
The Toy & Model Bus Handbook - Volume 1 - Early Diecasts
The Fire Brigade Handbook (fleet list of each local authority fire brigade)
The Fire Brigade Handbook - Special Appliances Volume 1
The Fire Brigade Handbook - Special Appliances Volume 2

Contents

In 1956 Liverpool added six Crossley-bodied Leyland Royal Tigers to the fleet for use on services to the Airport. These were bodied by Crossley and featured a raised rear portion to accomodate additional luggage.
Reg Wilson

The 1968 North West Bus Handbook

The 1968 North West Bus Handbook is one of the Bus Handbook Heritage series. It details the fleets of stage carriage and express coach operators that operated in the North West during 1968 in the period before the formation of the PTEs and the consequent demise of many long-establishedoperators.

British Bus Publishing,
The Vyne,
16 St Margaret's Drive
Wellington
Telford,
Shropshire TF1 3PH

Editor for *The 1968 North West Bus Handbook*: · Stewart J Brown

Acknowledgements:
We are grateful to David Donati, John Jones, Roy Marshall, Bill Potter, Steve Sanderson, Reg Wilson and the PSV Circle. The front cover photograph is by Bill Potter

ISBN 1 897990 65 0
Published by *British Bus Publishing*
The Vyne, 16 St Margaret's Drive, Wellington,
Telford, Shropshire, TF1 3PH
Evening orderline - 01952 255669 Fax - 01952 222397

Introduction

In 1968 Britain's bus industry was on the brink of major change, and nowhere would that be seen more clearly than in north-west England.

The Labour government of the day was committed to the co-ordination of public transport and in pursuing this worthwhile objective created four Passenger Transport Executives in England's biggest metropolitan areas outside London. Two of these were in the north-west - in Manchester and Merseyside.

The PTEs were to take over the municipal bus operations within their areas, and at a stroke a number of Lancashire's (and Cheshire's) colourful municipal fleets would disappear. As it happened, of course, the colour didn't disappear at a stroke - but disappear it did in the early part of the 1970s as the PTEs stamped their own identities on the operations they had absorbed.

There were changes afoot for the company operators too, with the imminent creation of a new state-owned National Bus Company which would take control of the fleets previously operated by British Electric Traction and the Transport Holding Company, more commonly referred to as the Tilling Group. BET, fearing for the future under a Labour government - and no doubt also concerned about having experienced two decades of declining passenger numbers - sold out to the THC in March 1968. Here, too, long-established liveries would vanish under a new corporate identity introduced by NBC.

Up to 1968 the bus industry in the north-west had enjoyed a long period of stability - as indeed it had elsewhere in the UK. A tight system of road service licensing controlled all aspects of bus and coach operation except private hires. Road service licences dictated routes, timetables and fares, and any alteration had to be approved by the traffic commissioners. There was no real competition between operators. Instead all sheltered behind the licensing system which protected their routes from any challenges.

Which meant that in most towns route networks changed but slowly, and long established bus services were often following the same roads as had the trams they had often replaced many years earlier. All that was to change, as the PTEs worked, slowly, towards integration.

Outside the metropolitan areas the reorganisation of local government in 1974 would bring further change, such as the merger of Blackburn and Darwen, or Lancaster and Morecambe, and the absorption by the expanded PTEs of a few more municipal fleets.

There were changes coming in operating practices too. In 1968 there were very few orders outstanding for front-engined half-cab buses. Most operators had, sometimes with reluctance, accepted the new rear-engined models which had first appeared almost a decade earlier. These were revolutionising the shape of bus fleets as modern-looking and invariably bigger buses ousted elderly half-cabs.

Bury required special buses for route 23T to Bolton where a weight limit provided restrictions. Four Leyland Titans joined the fleet in1967 and these carried East Lancs forward entrance bodywork.

A look at the lists in the pages which follow will highlight the variety which could be seen in the north-west in 1968, from late 1940s rear-entrance half-cab Titans through to ultra-modern two-door one-man-operated Panthers.

Crew-operation was still dominant - and remember that most Atlanteans and Fleetlines in service in 1968 still carried a conductor - but it was on the way out, even if that wasn't fully understood at the time.

Leyland, with its factories in the town which gave the marque its name, was far and away the biggest supplier of buses to fleets in the north-west as, once again, the fleet lists show. Leyland's problems lay in the future, and while its rear-engined models were far from trouble-free in its early days, the merger of Leyland and car-maker BMC in 1968 was heralded as the start of something big, the creation of a multi-faceted automotive empire which would conquer the world.

Local body builders East Lancs, Massey and Northern Counties had been key suppliers to the smaller municipal fleets, with Metro-Cammell doing fairly well out of the bigger operators. Massey was taken over by Northern Counties, which eventually consolidated on the Massey site at Pemberton.

Enthusiasts bemoaned the uniformity which they feared the PTEs would bring, and traditionalists were lamenting the impending loss of local liveries and the switch from front- to rear-engined buses. 1968 was the end of an era.
SJB

ACCRINGTON

Accrington Corporation Transport Department, 142 Blackburn Road, Accrington

In 1907 Accrington Corporation took over and electrified the steam tramway operation in the town. Bus operation started in 1928 with six Dennises. Double-deckers, also from Dennis, followed in 1929. The last trams ran in 1932, at which stage Accrington Corporation was running 48 buses, half of which were double-deckers.

Leylands dominated from 1930, but after receiving utility Guys during the war, that marque featured in orders in the 1950s and 1960s. From 1953 all new body orders were placed with East Lancs.

The future: In 1974 the operation became Hyndburn Borough Transport as a result of local government reorganisation. It then became Hyndburn Transport Ltd in 1986. In 1996 the operation was sold to Stagecoach and absorbed into the Ribble fleet.

An East Lancs-bodied Guy Arab IV of Accrington Corporation pulls out of the town's bus station. The Accrington fleet included both double- and single-deck Arabs as well as two Wulfrunians. *Roy Marshall*

In the 1960s deliveries were divided between Leyland and Guy with bodywork orders awarded to East Lancashire, although number 165 from the 1964 trio was assembled by associated company Neepsend. Pictured in the depot are Leyland 160 and Guy 163. *Bill Potter*

When it first adopted 30ft-long double-deckers Accrington continued to specify rear-entrance bodywork. The undertaking's first Leyland Titan PD3s, delivered in 1962, were 70-seaters with East Lancs bodies. *Stewart J Brown*

No.	Reg.	Type	Body	Seating	Year	
14	VTE778	Guy Arab LUF 6HLW	East Lancashire	B43R	1956	
15	VTE779	Guy Arab LUF 6HLW	East Lancashire	B43R	1956	
16	VTE780	Guy Arab LUF 6HLW	East Lancashire	B43R	1956	

17-24

	Leyland Tiger Cub PSUC1/13	East Lancashire	B43F	1962-65

17	381YTE	19	915TF	21	KTC334C	23	KTC336C	24	RTD506C
18	382YTE	20	916TF	22	KTC335C				

No.	Reg.	Type	Body	Seating	Year
25	MTJ925G	Bristol RESL6L	East Lancashire	B47F	1968
26	MTJ926G	Bristol RESL6L	East Lancashire	B47F	1968
27	MTJ927G	Bristol RESL6L	East Lancashire	B47F	1968
127	NTD589	Leyland Titan PD2/1	Leyland	H30/26R	1951
128	NTD590	Leyland Titan PD2/1	Leyland	H30/26R	1951

129-147

	Guy Arab IV 6LW	East Lancashire	H32/26R	1953-58

129	PTE193	134	STE763	138	354BTB	142	321DTB	145	324DTB
131	PTE191	135	STE764	139	355BTB	143	322DTB	146	387FTB
132	PTE192	136	STE765	140	356BTB	144	323DTB	147	388FTB
133	PTE195	137	STE766	141	357BTB				

No.	Reg.	Type	Body	Seating	Year
148	383FTJ	Leyland Titan PD2/31	East Lancashire	H32/26R	1958
149	384FTJ	Leyland Titan PD2/31	East Lancashire	H32/26R	1958
150	825KTB	Guy Arab IV 6LW	East Lancashire	H32/26R	1959
151	826KTB	Guy Arab IV 6LW	East Lancashire	H32/26R	1959
152	827KTB	Guy Arab IV 6LW	East Lancashire	H32/26R	1959
153	828KTB	Guy Arab IV 6LW	East Lancashire	H32/26R	1959
154	949RTB	Leyland Titan PD2/31	East Lancashire	H35/28R	1960
155	950RTB	Leyland Titan PD2/31	East Lancashire	H35/28R	1960
156	35VTF	Guy Wulfrunian 6LW	East Lancashire	H37/29R	1961
157	36VTF	Guy Wulfrunian 6LW	East Lancashire	H37/29R	1961

158-162

	Leyland Titan PD3A/1*	East Lancashire	H38/32R	1962-63	*161/2 are PD3A/2

158	417XTF	159	418XTF	160	914TF	161	9689TJ	162	9690TJ

No.	Reg.	Type	Body	Seating	Year
163	CTB557B	Guy Arab V 6LX	East Lancashire	H38/32R	1964
164	CTB558B	Guy Arab V 6LX	East Lancashire	H38/32R	1964
165	FTD643B	Guy Arab V 6LX	Neepsend	H38/32R	1964
166	CTB166E	Leyland Titan PD3A/2	East Lancashire	H41/31F	1967
167	CTB167E	Leyland Titan PD3A/2	East Lancashire	H41/31F	1967
168	CTB168E	Leyland Titan PD3A/2	East Lancashire	H41/31F	1967
169	CTB169E	Leyland Titan PD3A/2	East Lancashire	H41/31F	1967

On order: 3 Leyland Atlantean/East Lancashire and 2 Bristol RESL6L/East Lancashire
Livery: Dark blue, red and black.

The first forward-entrance buses for Accrington were four Leyland Titan PD3A/2s delivered in 1967. These were also the fleet's last half-cabs. Like the vast majority of Accrington's buses they had East Lancs bodies.
Roy Marshall

ASHTON-UNDER-LYNE

Ashton-under-Lyne Corporation Passenger Transport, Mossley Road, Ashton-u-Lyne

Municipal tramway operation in Ashton started in 1902. Joint working with the neighbouring SHMD and Manchester undertakings was a feature from the early days.

Motorbuses, two Guys, were introduced in 1923, followed by trolleybuses, eight Railless, in 1925. The last trams - which were replaced by trolleybuses - ran in 1938. At this time Ashton ran 14 trolleybuses and 30 motorbuses, with Crossley being the major supplier. A few Crossleys - both motorbuses and trolleybuses - were purchased after World War II, but most new postwar vehicles were Leyland Titans.

Trolleybus operation ceased at the end of 1966, at which time just eight remained in use on a joint service with Manchester.

The future: Ashton's bus operations were taken over by the SELNEC PTE in November 1969

The typical Ashton bus of the early 1960s was the Roe-bodied Leyland Titan PD2, a type which made up almost half of the fleet in 1968. Most were rear-entrance models although the last batch, delivered in 1965, had forward entrances. *Roy Marshall*

Ashton moved to high-capacity rear-engined buses in 1966 with the delivery of eight Atlanteans with 75-seat Roe-bodies. These were PDR1/2 models with drop-centre rear axles which allowed a step-free gangway for the full length of the lower deck. Number 49 is seen in central Manchester. *Roy Marshall*

1-10

Leyland Titan PD2/3 — Leyland — H30/26R 1950

1	LTC761	3	LTC763	5	LTC765	7	LTC767	9	LTC769
2	LTC762	4	LTC764	6	LTC766	8	LTC768	10	LTC770

11-17

Leyland Titan PD2/12 — Crossley — H32/28R 1955

11	UTB311	13	UTB313	15	UTB315	16	UTB316	17	UTB317
12	UTB312	14	UTB314						

18-41

Leyland Titan PD2/40 — Roe — H37/28R 1960-64

18	18NTD	23	23NTD	28	228YTB	33	338TF	38	DTJ138B
19	19NTD	24	224YTB	29	229YTB	34	334TF	39	DTJ139B
20	20NTD	25	225YTB	30	230YTB	35	335TF	40	DTJ140B
21	21NTD	26	226YTB	31	231YTB	36	336TF	41	DTJ141B
22	22NTD	27	227YTB	32	332TF	37	337TF		

42-46

Leyland Titan PD2/37 — Roe — H37/28F 1965

42	PTE942C	43	PTE943C	44	PTE944C	45	PTE945C	46	PTE946C

47-54

Leyland Atlantean PDR1/2 — Roe — H43/32F 1966

47	YTE847D	49	YTE849D	51	YTE851D	53	YTE853D	54	YTE854D
48	YTE848D	50	YTE850D	52	YTE852D				

55	CTC355E	Leyland Panther Cub PSRC1/1	East Lancashire	B43F	1967
56	CTC356E	Leyland Panther Cub PSRC1/1	East Lancashire	B43F	1967
65	XTC852	Guy Arab IV 5LW	Bond	H32/28R	1956
66	XTC853	Guy Arab IV 5LW	Bond	H32/28R	1956
68	XTC855	Guy Arab IV 5LW	Bond	H32/28R	1956

Livery: Blue and ivory

BARROW

Barrow-in-Furness Corporation Transport, Hindpool Road, Barrow

Steam-hauled trams were introduced to Barrow in July 1885, operated by Barrow-in-Furness Tramways Ltd. The system was taken over by BET in 1899, and electrified services started in 1904. The company's 24 trams and two trailers were taken over by the Corporation on 1 January 1920.

The Corporation introduced a bus service to feed the trams in August 1923, using two Chevrolets and a Ford. The first double-deckers, four Leyland Titan TD1s, were purchased in 1929, and in 1932 the trams were withdrawn, replaced by a fleet of 18 Crossley Condor double-deckers, half of which were diesel-powered, and the remainder of which were later converted to diesel.

Thereafter most new buses were Leylands, although the undertaking's first new postwar buses were 20 Crossley DD42s with Crossley bodywork - none of which lasted more than 10 years. From 1934 to 1951 all new buses were double-deckers, but few single-deckers were purchased in the 1950s and these were used to introduce one-man-operation in 1958.

The last new double-deckers were purchased in 1961. Subsequent additions to the Barrow fleet were dual-door one-man-operated Leyland Leopards.

The future: Barrow-in-Furness Corporation Transport became Barrow Borough Transport Ltd in 1986. It ceased operation in 1989 after facing strong competition from Ribble. The town is now served by Stagecoach Cumberland.

1-10			Leyland Titan PD2A/27		Massey			H37/27F	1961			
1	HEO271	3	HEO273	5	HEO275	7	HEO277	9	HEO279
2	HEO272	4	HEO274	6	HEO276	8	HEO278	10	HEO280

50-54			Leyland Leopard PSU3/1R		Strachan			B51D	1966	
50	BEO950D	51	BEO951D	52	BEO952D	53	BEO953D	54	BEO954D

55-59			Leyland Leopard PSU3/1R		Neepsend			B51D	1967	
55	EEO255E	56	EEO256E	57	EEO257E	58	EEO258E	59	EEO259E

60-64			Leyland Leopard PSU3A/2R		East Lancashire			B51D	1968	
60	GEO160G	61	GEO161G	62	GEO162G	63	GEO163G	64	GEO164G

66	BEO397	Leyland Royal Tiger PSU1/13	Massey	B40F	1955
67	EEO468	Leyland Tiger Cub PSUC1/1	Massey	DP37F	1959

68-73			Leyland Leopard L1		East Lancashire			B42D	1963	
68	JEO768	70	JEO770	71	JEO771	72	JEO772	73	JEO773
69	JEO769								

130-140			Leyland Titan PD2/3		Park Royal			H30/26R	1949	
130	EO9057	136	EO9063	137	EO9064	139	EO9066	140	EO9067
134	EO9061								

141-150 Leyland Titan PD2/3 Roe (1959-60) H31/28R 1950

| 141 | EO9171 | 143 | EO9173 | 145 | EO9175 | 147 | EO9177 | 149 | EO9179 |
| 142 | EO9172 | 144 | EO9174 | 146 | EO9176 | 148 | EO9178 | 150 | EO9180 |

151-160 Leyland Titan PD2/3 Park Royal H33/26R 1951

| 151 | EO9502 | 153 | EO9504 | 155 | EO9506 | 157 | EO9508 | 160 | EO9511 |
| 152 | EO9503 | 154 | EO9505 | 156 | EO9507 | 159 | EO9510 | | |

161-170 Leyland Titan PD2/40 Park Royal H33/28R 1958

| 161 | CEO948 | 163 | CEO950 | 165 | CEO952 | 167 | CEO954 | 169 | CEO956 |
| 162 | CEO949 | 164 | CEO951 | 166 | CEO953 | 168 | CEO955 | 170 | CEO957 |

Livery: Blue and cream.

Massey single-deck bodywork was relatively rare, but Barrow ran two Massey-bodied saloons. The older of the two was this 1955 Leyland Royal Tiger.
Michael Fowler

Barrow's fleet was 100 per cent Leyland in 1968, and included ten PD2 Titans that dated from 1950 but which had been rebodied by Roe ten years later. The new bodies were of an old style with almost square corners to the windows.
Reg Wilson

13

BIRKENHEAD

Birkenhead Corporation Transport, Laird Street, Birkenhead

Britain's first street tramway was started by the Birkenhead Street Railway Company in August 1860, running from Woodside Ferry to Birkenhead Park.

Electric tramway operation was introduced by Birkenhead Corporation in February 1901 over lines previously operated by the Birkenhead United Tramway, Omnibus and Carriage Co (successors to the original Birkenhead Street Railway Co) and the Wirral Tramways Co.

The Corporation's first buses, five Leylands, were purchased in 1919, and from 1925 buses started replacing trams. The last trams ran in July 1937. Most of the replacement buses were Leyland Lions and Titans, although Birkenhead did run an AEC Q double-decker from 1933 to 1940.

In the 1930s Leyland Titans dominated the fleet. During World War II Guys were added, and small numbers of Arabs were purchased until 1956. From 1957 the exposed-radiator Leyland Titan PD2 was Birkenhead's standard bus, although nine Daimler Fleetlines, the undertaking's first rear-engined buses, were purchased in 1964 and were followed by Atlanteans in 1968.

From the mid-1950s most Birkenhead buses had bodywork by Massey Bros of Wigan.

The future: Birkenhead Corporation's bus fleet was absorbed by the Merseyside PTE in December 1969.

The typical Birkenhead Titan had an exposed radiator, synchromesh gearbox and stylish Massey bodywork - there were 120 broadly similar buses in the fleet.
Roy Marshall

1-30   Leyland Titan PD2/40   Massey   H31/28R   1957-58

1	FCM991	4	FCM994	7	FCM997	10	FBG910	13	FBG913
2	FCM992	5	FCM995	8	FCM998	11	FBG911	14	FBG914
3	FCM993	6	FCM996	9	FBG909	12	FBG912	15	FBG915

16-30   Leyland Titan PD2/40   Massey   H33/28R   1958-60

16	HCM516	19	HCM519	22	HCM522	25	HCM525	28	HCM528
17	HCM517	20	HCM520	23	HCM523	26	HCM526	29	HCM529
18	HCM518	21	HCM521	24	HCM524	27	HCM527	30	HCM530

31-45   Leyland Titan PD2/40   Massey   H35/28R   1960-61

31	JBG531	34	JBG534	37	JBG537	40	JBG540	43	JBG543
32	JBG532	35	JBG535	38	JBG538	41	JBG541	44	JBG544
33	JBG533	36	JBG536	39	JBG539	42	JBG542	45	JBG545

46-60   Leyland Titan PD2/40   East Lancashire   H37/28R   1961

46	LCM446	49	LCM449	52	LCM452	55	LCM455	58	LCM458
47	LCM447	50	LCM450	53	LCM453	56	LCM456	59	LCM459
48	LCM448	51	LCM451	54	LCM454	57	LCM457	60	LCM460

61-75   Leyland Titan PD2/40   Massey   H35/30R   1962

61	MCM961	64	MCM964	67	MCM967	70	MCM970	73	MCM973
62	MCM962	65	MCM965	68	MCM968	71	MCM971	74	MCM974
63	MCM963	66	MCM966	69	MCM969	72	MCM972	75	MCM975

76-90   Leyland Titan PD2/40   Massey   H35/30R   1963

76	OCM976	79	OCM979	82	OCM982	85	OCM985	88	OCM988
77	OCM977	80	OCM980	83	OCM983	86	OCM986	89	OCM989
78	OCM978	81	OCM981	84	OCM984	87	OCM987	90	OCM990

91	RCM491	Leyland Leopard L2	Massey	B42D	1964
92	RCM492	Leyland Leopard L2	Massey	B42D	1964
93	RCM493	Leyland Leopard L2	Massey	B42D	1964
94	RCM494	Leyland Leopard L2	Massey	B42D	1964

101-109   Daimler Fleetline CRG6LX   Weymann   H44/33F   1964

101	RCM501	103	RCM503	105	RCM505	107	RCM507	109	RCM509
102	RCM502	104	RCM504	106	RCM506	108	RCM508		

110-139   Leyland Titan PD2/40   Massey   H36/30R   1965-66

110	BBG110C	116	BBG116C	122	BBG122C	128	DBG128D	134	DBG134D
111	BBG111C	117	BBG117C	123	BBG123C	129	DBG129D	135	DBG135D
112	BBG112C	118	BBG118C	124	BBG124C	130	DBG130D	136	DBG136D
113	BBG113C	119	BBG119C	125	DBG125D	131	DBG131D	137	DBG137D
114	BBG114C	120	BBG120C	126	DBG126D	132	DBG132D	138	DBG138D
115	BBG115C	121	BBG121C	127	DBG127D	133	DBG133D	139	DBG139D

140-154   Leyland Titan PD2/37   Massey   H36/30R   1967

140	GCM140E	143	GCM143E	146	GCM146E	149	GCM149E	152	GCM152E
141	GCM141E	144	GCM144E	147	GCM147E	150	GCM150E	153	GCM153E
142	GCM142E	145	GCM145E	148	GCM148E	151	GCM151E	154	GCM154E

155-167   Leyland Atlantean PDR1/1   Northern Counties   H44/33F   1968

155	LCM155G	158	LCM158G	161	LCM161G	164	LCM164G	166	LCM166G
156	LCM156G	159	LCM159G	162	LCM162G	165	LCM165G	167	LCM167G
157	LCM157G	160	LCM160G	163	LCM163G				

226-240		Guy Arab III 6LW		East Lancashire		H33/26R	1952		
226	BCM926	229	BCM929	232	BCM932	235	BCM935	238	BCM938
227	BCM927	230	BCM930	233	BCM933	236	BCM936	239	BCM939
228	BCM928	231	BCM931	234	BCM934	237	BCM937	240	BCM940

241-255		Guy Arab II 6LW		Massey (1953)		H31/28R	1944		
241	BG8556	244	BG8628	247	BG8631	250	BG8642	253	BG8645
242	BG8557	245	BG8629	248	BG8632	251	BG8643	254	BG8646
243	BG8558	246	BG8630	249	BG8641	252	BG8644	255	BG8647

256-265		Leyland Titan PD2/12		Weymann		H33/26R	1954		
256	CBG556	258	CBG558	260	CBG560	262	CBG562	264	CBG564
257	CBG557	259	CBG559	261	CBG561	263	CBG563	265	CBG565

266-270		Leyland Titan PD2/12		Ashcroft		H33/26R	1954		
266	CBG566	267	CBG567	268	CBG568	269	CBG569	270	CBG570

355-361		Guy Arab IV 6LW		Massey		H31/28R	1955		
355	DCM975	357	DCM977	359	DCM979	360	DCM980	361	DCM981
356	DCM976	358	DCM978						

362-366		Leyland Titan PD2/12		East Lancashire		H31/28R	1955		
362	DCM982	363	DCM983	364	DCM984	365	DCM985	366	DCM986

367-371		Leyland Titan PD2/12		Weymann Orion		H33/26R	1955		
367	DCM987	368	DCM988	369	DCM989	370	DCM990	371	DCM991

372-381		Guy Arab IV 6LW		Massey		H31/28R	1956		
372	EBG59	374	EBG61	376	EBG63	378	EBG750	380	EBG752
373	EBG60	375	EBG62	377	EBG64	379	EBG751	381	EBG753

382-386		Guy Arab IV 6LW		East Lancashire		H31/28R	1956		
382	EBG754	383	EBG755	384	EBG756	385	EBG757	386	EBG758

Livery: Blue and cream

Opposite: **Leylands dominated the Birkenhead fleet and included five Titans dating from 1954 with bodywork by local coachbuilder Ashcroft. Birkenhead's first rear-engined buses marked a return to Daimler after a 14 year break and were nine Fleetlines with Weymann bodies which entered service in 1964. They were the last Daimlers to be bought by Birkenhead. Its next rear-engined buses were Atlanteans.** *Reg Wilson*

In contrast to Birkenhead, neighbouring Wallasey was the first operator to put an Atlantean into service in December 1958, and had a fleet of 30 in operation by 1961. These had Metro-Cammell bodies and were the undertaking's last new double-deckers. The panel behind the driver - a unique Wallasey feature - carries an advert for the Pavilion Theatre. *Roy Marshall*

BLACKBURN

Blackburn Corporation Transport Department, Railway Road, Blackburn

In 1898 Blackburn Corporation took over the operation of the Blackburn and Over Darwen Tramways Co, doing so jointly with neighbouring Darwen Corporation. Electrification followed and by 1908 Blackburn Corporation had a fleet of 61 tramcars.

In 1929 the first buses were purchased - six Leyland Tigers and six Leyland Titans - and in 1931 the Corporation (jointly with Ribble) bought the Blackburn Bus Company. This added 10 buses to the Corporation fleet.

The first tramway withdrawal took place in 1938, by which time Blackburn's bus fleet numbered 51 vehicles, all Leylands. The Corporation's last tram ran in September 1949.

Two AEC Regents with East Lancs bodies were purchased in 1939. These were the undertaking's first and last AECs. They were also the first buses in the fleet with bodies by East Lancs, established in the town a few years earlier. It would be 1957 before a return was made to East Lancs bodywork - but from that point on it was Blackburn's standard choice.

Guys were allocated to the fleet during World War II and continued to be purchased until 1961. Leylands were also bought in the late 1940s, and from 1962 all new buses were of Leyland manufacture.

The future: When local government in England and Wales was reorganised in 1974, Blackburn Borough Council took over the bus operations of both Blackburn and Darwen Corporations. The operation became Blackburn Borough Transport Ltd in 1986, with the local authority retaining ownership.

Opposite: Blackburn's last Titans were two dozen PD2A/24s – a specification which embraced a Pneumocyclic gearbox and air brakes - and the last of these were delivered in 1964. They had bodywork built in the town by East Lancs. *Stewart J Brown/Bill Potter*

Blackburn ran a substantial fleet of Guys, including 30 Arab IVs. Most of these had Birmingham-style new-look fronts as on this 1957 bus, although the final batch, delivered in 1961, had the short-lived Johannesburg front. All had East Lancs bodies.
Roy Marshall

No.	Reg.	Chassis	Body	Seating	Year
9	BCB342	Leyland Tiger PS1	Crossley	B32F	1948
10	BCB343	Leyland Tiger PS1	Crossley	B32F	1948

11-18
Leyland Tiger Cub PSUC1/13 — East Lancashire — B45F — 1967

11	FCB11D	13	GBV13E	15	GBV15E	17	GBV17E	18	GBV18E
12	FCB12D	14	GBV14E	16	GBV16E				

21-44
Leyland Titan PD2A/24 — East Lancashire — H35/28R — 1962-64

21	PCB21	26	PCB26	31	PCB31	36	ABV36B	41	ABV41B
22	PCB22	27	PCB27	32	PCB32	37	ABV37B	42	ABV42B
23	PCB23	28	PCB28	33	ABV33B	38	ABV38B	43	ABV43B
24	PCB24	29	PCB29	34	ABV34B	39	ABV39B	44	ABV44B
25	PCB25	30	PCB30	35	ABV35B	40	ABV40B		

45-54
Leyland Atlantean PDR1A/1 — East Lancashire — H45/31F — 1968

45	KBV45F	47	KBV47F	49	KBV49F	51	KBV51F	53	KBV53F
46	KBV46F	48	KBV48F	50	KBV50F	52	KBV52F	54	KBV54F

86-94
Leyland Titan PD1 — Leyland/Salmesbury — H30/26R — 1947

86	BBV317	88	BBV319	90	BBV321	92	BBV323	94	BBV325
87	BBV318	89	BBV320	91	BBV322	93	BBV324		

106-118
Leyland Titan PD1A — Leyland — H30/26R — 1947-48

106	BBV901	109	BBV904	112	BBV907	114	BBV909	117	BBV912
107	BBV902	110	BBV905	113	BBV908	116	BBV911	118	BBV913
108	BBV903								

120-139
Guy Arab III 6LW — Crossley — H30/26R — 1949

120	CBV420	124	CBV424	129	CBV429	133	CBV433	137	CBV437
121	CBV421	125	CBV425	130	CBV430	134	CBV434	138	CBV438
122	CBV422	126	CBV426	131	CBV431	135	CBV435	139	CBV439
123	CBV423	127	CBV427	132	CBV432	136	CBV436		

140-157
Guy Arab IV 6LW — East Lancashire — H32/26R — 1957-58

140	HCB140	144	HCB144	148	HCB148	152	KBV152	155	KBV155
141	HCB141	145	HCB145	149	HCB149	153	KBV153	156	KBV156
142	HCB142	146	HCB146	150	KBV150	154	KBV154	157	KBV157
143	HCB143	147	HCB147	151	KBV151				

158-169
Guy Arab IV 6LW — East Lancashire — H35/28R — 1961

158	NCB158	161	NCB161	164	NCB164	166	NCB166	168	NCB168
159	NCB159	162	NCB162	165	NCB165	167	NCB167	169	NCB169
160	NCB160	163	NCB163						

On order: 12 Leyland Tiger Cub/East Lancashire ; Livery: Green and ivory.

Growing interest in one-man-operation saw Blackburn buy eight Leyland Tiger Cubs with East Lancs bodies in 1967, designed for operation without a conductor at a time when this was unusual in urban operation.
Roy Marshall

BLACKPOOL

Blackpool Corporation Transport Department, Bloomfield Road, Blackpool.

The Corporation took over the operation of the Blackpool Electric Tramways Co in September 1892, and expanded the system, which had only been in operation since 1885. In 1920 the Corporation acquired the Blackpool and Fleetwood Tramroad Co and its 41 trams.

Municipal bus operation commenced in 1921 with two Tilling-Stevens single-deckers. A double-decker from the same manufacturer was added to the fleet in 1922. By the end of 1926 there were 38 buses in operation, including half-a-dozen acquired with the business of a local operator, Smith.

The 1930s was a period of expansion and modernisation, with new streamlined trams - and buses to match. Most of the buses were Leyland Titans with fully-fronted centre-entrance bodywork built by Burlingham, who were based in Blackpool. When withdrawal of these buses took place in the late 1940s and early 1950s their replacements were 100 PD2 Titans, again with fully-fronted centre-entrance Burlingham bodies.

There was a scaling down of the tramway network in the 1960s, leaving only the sea-front service from Starr Gate to Fleetwood. And the buses became more conventional too, with post-1957 Titans having conventional rear-entrance bodies, albeit still with full-width cabs until 1965. These later Titans - both short PD2s and long PD3s - had Metro-Cammell Orion bodies, apart from the first five in 1957 which were the last Burlingham-bodied buses for Blackpool.

The future: In 1974 the undertaking became Blackpool Borough Transport, and in 1986 Blackpool Transport Services Ltd, still in local authority ownership. It purchased neighbouring Fylde Borough Transport in 1994.

From 1957 Blackpool abandoned centre-entrance bodywork, going instead for a more conventional layout albeit retaining a full-width cab. The first five of its new generation of rear entrance Titans had Burlingham bodies, but all subsequent deliveries were bodied by Metro-Cammell.
Roy Marshall

251-300   Leyland Titan PD2/5   Burlingham   FH29/23C   1950-51

251	EFV251	263	EFV263	274	EFV274	286	EFV286	295	EFV295
256	EFV256	265	EFV265	276	EFV276	289	EFV289	296	EFV296
257	EFV257	266	EFV266	277	EFV277	291	EFV291	298	EFV298
259	EFV259	269	EFV269	278	EFV278	293	EFV293	299	EFV299
261	EFV261	270	EFV270	280	EFV280	294	EFV294	300	EFV300
262	EFV262	271	EFV271	282	EFV282				

301-305   Leyland Titan PD2/21   Burlingham   FH35/28R   1957

301	LFV301	302	LFV302	303	LFV303	304	LFV304	305	LFV305

306-310   Leyland Titan PD2/21   Metro-Cammell   FH35/28R   1957

306	LFV306	307	LFV307	308	LFV308	309	LFV309	310	LFV310

311-350   Leyland Titan PD2/27   Metro-Cammell   FH35/28R   1958-59

311	NFV311	319	NFV319	327	NFV327	335	PFR335	343	PFR343
312	NFV312	320	NFV320	328	NFV328	336	PFR336	344	PFR344
313	NFV313	321	NFV321	329	NFV329	337	PFR337	345	PFR345
314	NFV314	322	NFV322	330	NFV330	338	PFR338	346	PFR346
315	NFV315	323	NFV323	331	PFR331	339	PFR339	347	PFR347
316	NFV316	324	NFV324	332	PFR332	340	PFR340	348	PFR348
317	NFV317	325	NFV325	333	PFR333	341	PFR341	349	PFR349
318	NFV318	326	NFV326	334	PFR334	342	PFR342	350	' PFR350

351-370   Leyland Titan PD3/1   Metro-Cammell   FH41/32R   1962

351	YFR351	355	YFR355	359	YFR359	363	YFR363	367	YFR367
352	YFR352	356	YFR356	360	YFR360	364	YFR364	368	YFR368
353	YFR353	357	YFR357	361	YFR361	365	YFR365	369	YFR369
354	YFR354	358	YFR358	362	YFR362	366	YFR366	370	YFR370

371-380   Leyland Titan PD3A/1   Metro-Cammell   FH41/30R   1964

371	371DFR	373	373DFR	375	375DFR	377	373DFR	379	379DFR
372	372DFR	374	374DFR	376	376DFR	378	374DFR	380	380DFR

381-500   Leyland Titan PD3A/1   Metro-Cammell   H41/30R   1964-65

381	CFR581C	385	CFR585C	389	CFR589C	393	CFR593C	397	CFR597C
382	CFR582C	386	CFR586C	390	CFR590C	394	CFR594C	398	CFR598C
383	CFR583C	387	CFR587C	391	CFR591C	395	CFR595C	399	CFR599C
384	CFR584C	388	CFR588C	392	CFR592C	396	CFR596C	500	CFR600C

501-525   Leyland Titan PD3A/1   Metro-Cammell   H41/30R   1967

501	HFR501E	506	HFR506E	511	HFR511E	516	HFR516E	521	HFR521E
502	HFR502E	507	HFR507E	512	HFR512E	517	HFR517E	522	HFR522E
503	HFR503E	508	HFR508E	513	HFR513E	518	HFR518E	523	HFR523E
504	HFR504E	509	HFR509E	514	HFR514E	519	HFR519E	524	HFR524E
505	HFR505E	510	HFR510E	515	HFR515E	520	HFR520E	525	HFR525E

526-540   Leyland Titan PD3/11   Metro-Cammell   H41/30R   1968

526	LFR526F	529	LFR529F	532	LFR532F	535	LFR535F	538	LFR538G
527	LFR527F	530	LFR530F	533	LFR533F	536	LFR536F	539	LFR539G
528	LFR528F	531	LFR531F	534	LFR534F	537	LFR537F	540	LFR540G

Opposite, top:- **The tram fleet was renumbered during 1968 with 280 becoming 680. The year also saw the withdrawal of the first Coronation car, which had proved to be expensive on maintenance and power.**
Bill Potter
Opposite, bottom: **The classic Blackpool bus for many years was the Leyland Titan with fully-fronted centre-entrance bodywork. The last of these flamboyant buses were 100 PD2s which were bodied by local coachbuilder Burlingham, and a few of these survived until the late 1960s.** *Reg Wilson*

Trams

600-607

		English Electric M4d		English Electric		OST56C	1934-35		
600	601	602	603	604	605	606	607		

608-620

		English Electric M4d		Blackpool Corporation (1987)		ST52D	1973		
608	610	612	614	615	616	617	618	619	620
609	611	613							

621-638

		EMB M4d		Brush		ST48C	1937		
621	623	626	630	632	633	634	636	637	638
622	625	627	631						

641-664

		Maley & Taunton M4d		Roberts		ST56C	1953		
641	644	647	650	653	655	657	659	661	663
642	645	648	651	654	656	658	660	662	664
643	646	649	652						

671-677

		English Electric, 1935 M4s		English Electric		ST53C	1960
671	672	673	674	675	676	677	

678		English Electric, 1935 M4d		English Electric		ST48C	1960
679		English Electric, 1935 M4d		English Electric		ST48C	1960
680		English Electric, 1935 M4d		English Electric		ST48C	1960

681-687

		Maley & Taunton M4d		MCW		ST61C	1960
681	682	683	684	685	686	687	

700-726

		English Electric M4d		English Electric		DT54/40C	1934-35		
700	703	706	709	712	715	718	721	723	725
701	704	707	710	713	716	719	722	724	726
702	705	708	711	714	717	720			

731		Dick Kerr M4s		Blackpool Corporation		32-seat	1960	*Blackpool Belle*
732		Dick Kerr M4s		Blackpool Corporation		48-seat	1960	*Rocket*
733		English Electric M4d		Blackpool Corporation		35-seat	1962	*Western Train*
734		Dick Kerr B4s		Blackpool Corporation		60-seat	1962	*Train coach*
735		English Electric M4d		Blackpool Corporation		57/42	1963	*Hovertram*
736		Dick Kerr M4d		Blackpool Corporation		71-seat	1965	*Frigate*

On order: 15 AEC Swift/Marshall; Livery: Cream and green

Blackpool finally gave up on full-width cabs in 1964, and from 1965 its Titans had standard Metro-Cammell Orion bodies. A 1968 example waits in St Annes on the service between the two towns which was operated jointly with Lytham St Annes Corporation.
Roy Marshall

BOLTON TRANSPORT

County Borough of Bolton Transport Department, 147 Bradshawgate, Bolton

Bolton Corporation took over the horse tramway operation of E Holden & Co in 1899, and electrified - and extended - the services. It was the first municipal bus operator in north-west England, running a steam bus in 1904-05, and again in 1907. Regular bus operation got under way in 1924 with nine Leylands. All subsequent new buses until World War II were Leylands - except for a solitary AEC Q in 1933. Double-deckers were operated from 1927.

In 1936 the decision was made to replace trams with buses, although the war slowed this process and the last trams survived until March 1947. These were replaced by a fleet of 75 Crossley DD42s. After buying 130 Leyland Titans in 1948-49 (and smaller numbers in 1955-56) Bolton's new bus orders also included Daimlers in 1957-58 and AECs in 1961, although from 1962 Leyland was once again the sole supplier.

Bolton was an early user of the Atlantean, standardising on it from 1963. General manager Ralph Bennett had a hand in the design of an attractive style of body for Bolton's new-generation buses, which was built by East Lancs.

An unusual quirk of history saw Bolton Corporation owning four trolleybuses which were operated on its behalf by South Lancashire Transport - with no external indication that they were Bolton-owned buses. This arrangement came to an end in 1956.

The future: In November 1969 Bolton Corporation Transport was absorbed by the SELNEC PTE.

9	GWH516	Leyland Royal Tiger PSU1/14	East Lancashire	B43F	1955	
10	JBN141	Leyland Royal Tiger PSU1/13	Bond	B44F	1956	
12	UWH322	Leyland Leopard L2	East Lancashire	DP41F	1962	
14	YBN14	Leyland Leopard PSU3/4R	East Lancashire	B49D	1964	
15	YBN15	Leyland Leopard PSU3/4R	East Lancashire	B49D	1964	
16	YBN16	Leyland Leopard L2	East Lancashire	B43D	1964	
17	YBN17	Leyland Leopard L2	East Lancashire	B43D	1964	

51-65				Leyland Titan PD2/13		Metro-Cammell		H31/27R	1955		
51	GWH501	54	GWH504	57	GWH507	60	GWH510	63	GWH513		
52	GWH502	55	GWH505	58	GWH508	61	GWH511	64	GWH514		
53	GWH503	56	GWH506	59	GWH509	62	GWH512	65	GWH515		

66	JBN140	Leyland Titan PD2/12	Bond	H32/28R	1955

67-75				Leyland Titan PD2/13		Bond		H33/27R	1955		
67	JBN143	69	JBN145	71	JBN147	73	JBN149	75	JBN151		
68	JBN144	70	JBN146	72	JBN148	74	JBN150				

76-84				Leyland Titan PD2/13		Metro-Cammell		H33/27R	1956		
76	JBN152	78	JBN154	80	JBN156	82	JBN158	84	JBN160		
77	JBN153	79	JBN155	81	JBN157	83	JBN159				

Bolton specified full-width cabs on a small number of buses in 1961-62. These included 10 PD2/27 Titans with 62-seat Metro-Cammell bodies. *Roy Marshall*

85-94
Daimler CVG6 — East Lancashire — H35/28R — 1957

85	KWH565	**87**	KWH567	**89**	KWH569	**91**	KWH571	**93**	KWH573
86	KWH566	**88**	KWH568	**90**	KWH570	**92**	KWH572	**94**	KWH574

95-105
Daimler CVG6 — Metro-Cammell — H34/28R — 1957

95	KWH575	**98**	KWH578	**100**	KWH580	**102**	KWH582	**104**	KWH584
96	KWH576	**99**	KWH579	**101**	KWH581	**103**	KWH583	**105**	KWH585
97	KWH577								

106-112
Daimler CVG6-30 — Metro-Cammell — H41/33R — 1958

106	MBN161	**108**	MBN163	**110**	MBN165	**111**	MBN166	**112**	MBN167
107	MBN162	**109**	MBN164						

113-122
Leyland Titan PD3/5 — East Lancashire — H41/33R — 1958

113	MBN168	**115**	MBN170	**117**	MBN172	**119**	MBN174	**121**	MBN176
114	MBN169	**116**	MBN171	**118**	MBN173	**120**	MBN175	**122**	MBN177

123-127
Leyland Titan PD2/37 — Metro-Cammell — H34/28R — 1959

123	NBN431	**124**	NBN432	**125**	NBN433	**126**	NBN434	**127**	NBN435

128-132
Leyland Titan PD3/4 — East Lancashire — H41/32F — 1959

128	NBN436	**129**	NBN437	**130**	NBN438	**131**	NBN439	**132**	NBN440

Opposite: **Pictured at the town's central bus station off Moor Lane is a 1956 Metro-Cammell-bodied Leyland Titan on lay over from a Hayward Schools duplicate that supplemented the Atlantean service.** *Bill Potter* **Bolton was among the pioneers in developing a new style for rear-engined double-deckers with improved body designs which included the use of polished mouldings and a revised livery layout. A 1968 East Lancs-bodied Atlantean in Bury shows what was achieved. Note the translucent roof panels, designed to make the upper deck brighter, a feature also to be found on earlier Titan models for Bolton.** *Reg Wilson*

Bond of Wythenshawe won small numbers of orders in the north-west the mid-1950s, including 10 double-deckers on Leyland Titan chassis for Bolton Transport in 1955. Pictured here is 66, which carries the Crook Street depot code in the cab. Bolton also took a Bond single-deck body on a Royal Tiger. *Roy Marshall*

133-142

Leyland Titan PD2/27   Metro-Cammell   FH35/27F   1961

133	PBN651	135	PBN653	137	PBN655	139	PBN657	141	PBN659
134	PBN652	136	PBN654	138	PBN656	140	PBN658	142	PBN660

143-150

Daimler CVG6-30   East Lancashire   H41/32F   1960

143	PBN661	145	PBN663	147	PBN665	149	PBN667	150	PBN668
144	PBN662	146	PBN664	148	PBN666				

151-161

Leyland Titan PD3/4   East Lancashire   H41/32F   1961

151	SBN751	154	SBN754	156	SBN756	158	SBN758	160	SBN760
152	SBN752	155	SBN755	157	SBN757	159	SBN759	161	SBN761
153	SBN753								

162-167

AEC Regent V 2D3RA   Metro-Cammell   H40/32F   1961

162	SBN762	164	SBN764	165	SBN765	166	SBN766	167	SBN767
163	SBN763								

168-176

Leyland Titan PD3A/2   East Lancashire   FH41/32F   1962

168	UBN901	170	UBN903	172	UBN905	174	UBN907	176	UBN909
169	UBN902	171	UBN904	173	UBN906	175	UBN908		

177-184

Leyland Titan PD3A/2   Metro-Cammell   FH41/31F   1962

177	UBN910	179	UBN912	181	UBN914	183	UBN916	184	UBN917
178	UBN911	180	UBN913	182	UBN915				

185-192

Leyland Atlantean PDR1/1   East Lancashire   H45/33F   1963

185	UWH185	187	UWH187	189	UWH189	191	UWH191	192	UWH192
186	UWH186	188	UWH188	190	UWH190				

193-199   Leyland Atlantean PDR1/1   Metro-Cammell   H43/35F   1963

193	UWH193	195	UWH195	197	UWH197	198	UWH198	199	UWH199
194	UWH194	196	UWH196						

200-218   Leyland Atlantean PDR1/1 ·   East Lancashire*   H45/33F   1964-65
*204-6/11 bodywork by Neepsend

200	ABN200B	204	ABN204B	208	ABN208B	212	ABN212C	216	ABN216C
201	ABN201B	205	ABN205B	209	ABN209B	213	ABN213C	217	ABN217C
202	ABN202B	206	ABN206B	210	ABN210B	214	ABN214C	218	ABN218C
203	ABN203B	207	ABN207B	211	ABN211B	215	ABN215C		

219-226   Leyland Atlantean PDR1/1   Metro-Cammell   H45/32F   1965

219	ABN219C	221	ABN221C	223	ABN223C	225	ABN225C	226	ABN226C
220	ABN220C	222	ABN222C	224	ABN224C				

227-241   Leyland Atlantean PDR1/1   East Lancashire   H45/33F   1965-66

227	FBN227C	230	FBN230C	233	FBN233C	236	FBN236C	239	FBN239D
228	FBN228C	231	FBN231C	234	FBN234C	237	FBN237D	240	FBN240C
229	FBN229C	232	FBN232C	235	FBN235D	238	FBN238C	241	FBN241C

242-271   Leyland Atlantean PDR1/1   East Lancashire   H45/33F   1966-67

242	GBN242D	248	GBN248D	254	GBN254D	260	HWH260F	266	HWH266F
243	GBN243D	249	GBN249D	255	GBN255D	261	HWH261F	267	HWH267F
244	GBN244D	250	GBN250D	256	GBN256D	262	HWH262F	268	HWH268F
245	GBN245D	251	GBN251D	257	HWH257F	263	HWH263F	269	HWH269F
246	GBN246D	252	GBN252D	258	HWH258F	264	HWH264F	270	HWH270F
247	GBN247D	253	GBN253D	259	HWH259F	265	HWH265F	271	HWH271F

272-286   Leyland Atlantean PDR1A/1   East Lancashire   H45/33F   1968

272	MWH272G	275	MWH275G	278	MWH278G	281	MWH281G	284	MWH284G
273	MWH273G	276	MWH276G	279	MWH279G	282	MWH282G	285	MWH285G
274	MWH274G	277	MWH277G	280	MWH280G	283	MWH283G	286	MWH286G

351-450   Leyland Titan PD2/4   Leyland   H32/26R   1948-49

351	CWH701	357	CWH707	363	CWH713	401	DBN304	431	DBN334
352	CWH702	358	CWH708	364	CWH714	410	DBN313	435	DBN338
353	CWH703	359	CWH709	390	CWH740	419	DBN322	439	DBN342
354	CWH704	360	CWH710	397	CWH747	422	DBN325	441	DBN344
355	CWH705	361	CWH711	398	CWH748	423	DBN326	443	DBN346
356	CWH706	362	CWH712	400	CWH750	429	DBN332	444	DBN347

Livery: Cream and maroon

Up to 1965 Bolton had divided itsbody orders between East Lancashire and Metro-Cammell. The MCW design on Bolton's Atlanteans blended the basic shape of the Liverpool design with translucent roof panels and an interior to Bolton design. The upper destination blind was changed from red to green background after it was found to be classed as displaying a red front light at night. *Roy Marshall*

BURNLEY, COLNE & NELSON JTC

Burnley, Colne & Nelson Joint Transport Committee, Queensgate, Burnley

The Burnley, Colne & Nelson Joint Transport Committee came into operation on 1 April 1933, taking over the municipal bus and tram fleets of the three towns.

Burnley, with some 70 trams 47 buses, was the biggest of BC&N's constituents. The buses were mainly Leyland Lions, but there were also 16 central-entrance AEC Regent and Crossley Condor double-deckers. Burnley Corporation had operated trams from 1901 and buses from 1924.

Colne Corporation contributed 24 single-deck buses and 10 trams to the BC&N fleet. It had been running trams since 1914, and had started regular bus operation in 1923. Nelson was the smallest of the three BC&N constituents, running 15 Leyland Lions and nine trams.

Later in 1933 BC&N, jointly with Ribble, took over part of the business of Laycock of Barnoldswick, which added seven Maudslays to the fleet. The tramway system was closed in 1935, being replaced by Leyland Titans.

Most postwar additions to the BC&N fleet were Leylands and included, in 1955, the last new half-cab single-deckers for an English fleet. These were Leyland Tiger PS2s with rear-entrance East Lancs bodies.

The future: Local government reorganisation in 1974 saw Colne and Nelson being combined as the Borough of Pendle; BC&N in consequence became the Burnley & Pendle JTC. In 1986 it was reformed as the Burnley & Pendle Transport Co Ltd. In 1996 Stagecoach bought Pendle's share of the company, quickly followed by Burnley's share. Management of the company then passed to Ribble, although it remains a separate subsidiary trading as Stagecoach Burnley & Pendle.

21-26		Leyland Tiger Cub PSUC1/1		East Lancashire		B43F		1959	
21	HHG21	23	HHG23	24	HHG24	25	HHG25	26	HHG26
22	HHG22								

36-49		Leyland Tiger PS2/14		East Lancashire		B39F		1953-55	
36	BHG755	39	CHG539	42	CHG542	45	CHG545	48	DHG48
37	BHG756	40	CHG540	43	CHG543	46	CHG546	49	DHG49
38	BHG757	41	CHG541	44	CHG544	47	DHG47			

Opposite, top:- **In 1968, the Leyland Panther was the latest single-deck from Leyland being marketed as the way ahead, BCN took ten in that year.** *Bill Potter*
Opposite, bottom:- **Pictured while performing training duties is Northern Counties-bodied Leyland Titan from 1962. The advert indicates that the picture was taken before all-digit telephone numbers.** *Bill Potter*

Burnley, Colne & Nelson standardised on the forward-entrance PD2A/27 for its double-deck fleet in the 1960s, taking 26 between 1962 and 1967 with bodywork divided between Northern Counties, as on this 1962 bus, and East Lancs. All were 64-seaters. The first is seen leaving Burnley bus station. *Roy Marshall*

50-73

Leyland Tiger Cub PSUC1/11 — East Lancashire — B43F — 1963-67

50	NHG550	55	NHG555	60	BHG360C	65	BCW465B	70	FHG570E
51	NHG551	56	PCW956	61	BHG361C	66	BCW466B	71	FHG571E
52	NHG552	57	PCW957	62	BHG362C	67	BCW467B	72	FHG572E
53	NHG553	58	PCW958	63	BCW463B	68	BHG368C	73	FHG573E
54	NHG554	59	PCW959	64	BHG364C	69	BCW469B		

74-83

Leyland Panther PSUR1/1R — Northern Counties — B50F — 1968

74	HHG74F	76	HHG76F	78	HHG78F	80	HHG80F	82	HHG82F
75	HHG75F	77	HHG77F	79	HHG79F	81	HHG81F	83	HHG83F

142-153

Leyland Titan PD2/1 — Leyland — H30/26R — 1949

142	ACW562	145	ACW621	148	ACW640	150	ACW642	152	ACW644
143	ACW563	146	ACW622	149	ACW641	151	ACW643	153	ACW645
144	ACW564	147	ACW623						

177	HG9418	Leyland Titan PD2/3	Leyland	H30/26R	1947
178	HG9419	Leyland Titan PD2/3	Leyland	H30/26R	1947
179	HG9917	Leyland Titan PD2/3	Northern Counties	H31/26R	1948
180	HG9918	Leyland Titan PD2/3	Northern Counties	H31/26R	1948
182	HG9920	Leyland Titan PD2/3	Northern Counties	H31/26R	1948

183-188

Leyland Titan PD2/3 — Leyland — H32/25R — 1949

183	ACW142	185	ACW144	186	ACW145	187	ACW146	188	ACW147
184	ACW143								

189-196

Leyland Titan PD2/3 — East Lancashire — H31/26R — 1949

189	ACW333	191	ACW335	193	ACW558	195	ACW560	196	ACW561
190	ACW334	192	ACW336	194	ACW559					

Burnley, Colne & Nelson ran a varied single-deck fleet which included Tigers and Tiger Cubs. Two dozen of the latter joined the fleet between 1963 and 1967, all with 43-seat East Lancs bodies. *Reg Wilson*

197-212

Guy Arab III 6LW*   East Lancashire   H31/26R   1950-51   *204 is Arab III 6DG

197	AHG637	201	AHG640	204	AHG643	207	AHG646	210	AHG649
198	AHG638	202	AHG641	205	AHG644	208	AHG647	211	AHG650
199	AHG639	203	AHG642	206	AHG645	209	AHG648	212	AHG651
200	AHG347								

213-231

Leyland Titan PD2/12   East Lancashire   H34/26R*   1953-56   *213-8 are H31/26R

213	BHG749	217	BHG753	221	DHG221	225	EHG825	229	EHG829
214	BHG750	218	BHG754	222	DHG222	226	EHG826	230	EHG830
215	BHG751	219	DHG219	223	DHG223	227	EHG827	231	EHG831
216	BHG752	220	DHG220	224	DHG224	228	EHG828		

232-237

Leyland Titan PD3/6   East Lancashire   H41/32F   1959-61

| 232 | HHG32 | 234 | LHG534 | 235 | LHG535 | 236 | LHG536 | 237 | LHG537 |
| 233 | HHG33 | | | | | | | | |

238-247

Leyland Titan PD2A/27   Northern Counties   H37/27F   1962-64

| 238 | NHG538 | 240 | NHG540 | 242 | PCW942 | 244 | PCW944 | 246 | PCW946 |
| 239 | NHG539 | 241 | NHG541 | 243 | PCW943 | 245 | PCW945 | 247 | PCW947 |

248-252

Leyland Titan PD2A/27   East Lancashire   H37/27F   1965

| 248 | CHG548C | 249 | CHG549C | 250 | CHG550C | 251 | CHG551C | 252 | CHG552C |

253-257

Leyland Titan PD2A/27   Northern Counties   H37/27F   1965

| 253 | DCW353C | 254 | DCW354C | 255 | DCW355C | 256 | DCW356C | 257 | DCW357C |

258-263

Leyland Titan PD2A/27   East Lancashire   H37/27F   1967

| 258 | FHG158E | 260 | FHG160E | 261 | FHG161E | 262 | FHG162E | 263 | FHG163E |
| 259 | FHG159E | | | | | | | | |

On order: 5 Bristol RESL6/East Lancashire and 5 Bristol RESL6/Northen Counties.
Livery: Cream and maroon.

The 1968 North West Bus Handbook

BURY

Bury Corporation Transport, Rochdale Road, Bury

Bury Corporation started running electric trams in 1903 and took over the operations of the Bury, Rochdale and Oldham Steam Tramway Co in the town. Five Leylands introduced buses to the fleet in 1925, and in 1927 services were introduced to Burnley and to Rochdale, operated jointly with Rawtenstall and Rochdale respectively. Tramway abandonment started in 1933 and was completed in 1949.

In the early 1930s a mixed fleet was operated which included AEC, Crossley, Daimler, Dennis and Leyland chassis. From 1935 Leyland would be the main supplier. Unusual types in the postwar fleet came from Guy. Two 20-seat Wolf single-deckers were bought for a route to Nangreaves in 1948, while a Wulfrunian in 1960 proved as unsuccessful here as the model did elsewhere, being sold in 1963.

The future: Bury's bus operations were taken over by the SELNEC PTE in November 1969.

81-86		AEC Reliance MU3RV	Weymann		B43F	1957			
81	FEN81	83	FEN83	84	FEN84	85	FEN85	86	FEN86
82	FEN82								

87	TEN887	AEC Reliance 2MU3RV	Alexander Y	B43F	1964
88	TEN988	AEC Reliance 2MU3RA	Alexander Y	B43F	1964
89	FEN89E	Daimler Fleetline CRG6LX	East Lancashire	B41D	1967
90	FEN90E	Daimler Fleetline CRG6LX	East Lancashire	B41D	1967
91	FEN91E	Daimler Fleetline CRG6LX	East Lancashire	B41D	1967

102-116		Leyland Atlantean PDR1/1	Metro-Cammell		H41/33F	1963			
102	REN102	105	REN105	108	REN108	111	REN111	114	REN114
103	REN103	106	REN106	109	REN109	112	REN112	115	REN115
104	REN104	107	REN107	110	REN110	113	REN113	116	REN116

117-131		Daimler Fleetline CRG6LX	Alexander A		H43/31F	1964			
117	TEN117	120	TEN120	123	TEN123	126	TEN126	129	TEN129
118	TEN118	121	TEN121	124	TEN124	127	TEN127	130	TEN130
119	TEN119	122	TEN122	125	TEN125	128	TEN128	131	TEN131

132-143		Daimler Fleetline CRG6LX	East Lancashire		H45/31F	1965-68			
132	AEN832C	135	AEN835C	138	HEN538F	140	HEN540F	142	HEN542F
133	AEN833C	136	AEN836C	139	HEN539F	141	HEN541F	143	HEN543F
134	AEN834C	137	AEN837C						

152-174		Leyland Titan PD2/4	Weymann		H30/26R	1949-50			
152	EN9552	159	EN9959	162	EN9962	167	EN9967	174	EN9974
158	EN9958	160	EN9960	163	EN9963	169	EN9969		

176	BEN176	AEC Regent III 9613A	Weymann	H30/26R	1952
177	BEN177	AEC Regent III 9613A	Weymann	H30/26R	1952

Rear-engined buses arrived in Bury in 1963 with a batch of 15 Leyland Atlanteans with Metro-Cammell bodies similar to those being supplied to Liverpool, but with a number of detail differences - most notably the absence of Liverpool's polished skirt mouldings. Pictured on route 36 is 106, REN106. *Roy Marshall*

178-186

		Leyland Titan PD2/3		Weymann		H30/26R	1953			
178	BEN178	180	BEN180	182	BEN182	184	BEN184	186	BEN186	
179	BEN179	181	BEN181	183	BEN183	185	BEN185			

187	FEN587E	Leyland Titan PD2/37	East Lancashire	H37/28F	1967
188	FEN588E	Leyland Titan PD2/37	East Lancashire	H37/28F	1967
189	FEN589E	Leyland Titan PD2/37	East Lancashire	H37/28F	1967
190	FEN590E	Leyland Titan PD2/37	East Lancashire	H37/28F	1967

201-225

		Leyland Titan PD3/6		Weymann		H41/32R	1958-59			
201	GEN201	206	GEN206	211	GEN211	216	GEN216	221	GEN221	
202	GEN202	207	GEN207	212	GEN212	217	GEN217	222	GEN222	
203	GEN203	208	GEN208	213	GEN213	218	GEN218	223	GEN223	
204	GEN204	209	GEN209	214	GEN214	219	GEN219	224	GEN224	
205	GEN205	210	GEN210	215	GEN215	220	GEN220	225	GEN225	

Livery: Apple green and primrose

CHESTER

City of Chester Transport, Station Road, Chester

In 1902 Chester Corporation took over the horse trams of the Chester Tramways Co, electrifying the system in 1903. The 18 electric cars were replaced by 20 new AEC motorbuses, the Corporation's first, in 1930. These comprised 10 Regals and 10 Regents. By 1939 the fleet numbered 30 buses.

In 1942 Chester received two utility Guy Arabs, and this marque would feature in new bus orders until the close of the 1960s, although there were also some Daimlers and Fodens in the postwar vehicle intake. For two decades from 1946 most of Chester's buses were bodied by Massey of Wigan.

The future: Chester City Transport became a limited company in 1986, still owned by the city council.

1	RFM641	Guy Arab IV 6LW	Massey	H30/26R	1953
2	RFM642	Guy Arab IV 6LW	Massey	H30/26R	1953
3	RFM643	Guy Arab IV 6LW	Massey	H30/26R	1953
4	RFM644	Guy Arab IV 6LW	Guy/Park Royal	H30/26R	1954
5	RFM645	Guy Arab IV 6LW	Guy/Park Royal	H30/26R	1954
6	RFM646	Guy Arab IV 6LW	Guy/Park Royal	H30/26R	1954

Standardisation on Guys at Chester started in 1953 with an order for six Arab IVs. The last three of these had Guy bodywork built on Park Royal frames and were among the last examples of this type of collaboration between the two manufacturers. *Roy Marshall*

A batch of seven Arab IVs for Chester in 1961-62 had the rare Johannesburg-style bonnet and were the first forward-entrance buses in the fleet. Massey built the 73-seat body. *Roy Marshall*

7-12
Guy Arab IV 6LW — Massey — H30/26R — 1954-55

7	UFM858	9	UFM860	10	UFM861	11	UFM862	12	UFM863
8	UFM859								

13-23
Guy Arab IV 5LW — Massey — H32/26R* — 1955-57 — *19-23 are H32/28R

13	XFM521	16	XFM524	18	XFM526	20	714CFM	22	716CFM
14	XFM522	17	XFM525	19	713CFM	21	715CFM	23	717CFM
15	XFM523								

24-30
Guy Arab IV 6LW — Massey — H41/32F — 1961-62

24	324VFM	26	326VFM	28	328YFM	29	329YFM	30	330YFM
25	325VFM	27	327YFM						

31-41
Guy Arab V 6LW — Massey — H41/32F — 1963-66

31	4831FM	34	4834FM	36	FFM136C	38	FFM138C	40	LFM140D
32	4832FM	35	FFM135C	37	FFM137C	39	LFM139D	41	LFM141D
33	4833FM								

46	FFM278	Guy Arab II 5LW	Massey(1953)	H30/26R	1943	
51	LTV700	AEC Regal III 9621E	East Lancashire	B35R	1951	Nottingham City Transport, 1963
52	LFM152D	Leyland Tiger Cub PSUC1/11	Massey	B40D	1966	
53	RFM453F	Leyland Tiger Cub PSUC1/11	Massey	B40D	1967	
54	XFM54G	Leyland Tiger Cub PSUC1/11	Massey	B40D	1968	
55	FFM299	Guy Arab II 5LW	Massey(1952)	H30/26R	1944	
56	DTR907	Guy Arab II 6LW	Park Royal	H30/26R	1946	Southampton Corporation, 1959
57	DTR911	Guy Arab II 6LW	Park Royal	H30/26R	1946	Southampton Corporation, 1959
77	MFM556	Foden PVD6G	Massey	H30/26R	1950	
78	MFM557	Foden PVD6G	Massey	H30/26R	1950	

Livery: Maroon and ivory

The 1968 North West Bus Handbook

CUMBERLAND

Cumberland Motor Services Ltd, Tangier Street, Whitehaven

The Whitehaven Motor Service Co was formed in 1912, running two charabancs. By 1920 it had 17 vehicles, and the British Automobile Traction Co took a 50 per cent stake in the company. It was renamed Cumberland Motor Services in the following year. The bus station which it built in Workington in 1926 is thought to be the first purpose-built covered bus station in England.

The company's first new double-decker, a Guy, was delivered in 1927, but it was to Leyland that Cumberland turned for future double-deckers, starting with TD1 Titans in 1929. Leyland supplied most of Cumberland's new buses in the 1930s, although it also bought small Commers for deep rural routes.

BAT was reconstructed in 1928 with Tilling involvement, becoming the Tilling & British Automobile Traction Co. This arrangement came to an end in 1942, and Cumberland then became a Tilling group subsidiary. By this time the fleet numbered 150 vehicles. Leylands continued to be purchased after World War II, but from 1954 standard Tilling group Bristols joined the fleet.

The future: Cumberland became a subsidiary of the National Bus Company which took over the former Tilling group's bus operations on 1 January 1969. It was privatised in 1987, being sold to Stagecoach.

150-154		Leyland Royal Tiger PSU1/13		Eastern Coach Works		B45F	1952		
150	LAO144	151	LAO145	152	LAO146	153	LAO147	154	LAO148
155-161		Leyland Royal Tiger PSU1/13		Leyland		B44F	1953		
155	MAO107	157	MAO108	159	MAO111	160	MAO110	161	MAO112
156	MAO106	158	MAO109						
162-166		Leyland Royal Tiger PSU1/13		Eastern Coach Works		B45F	1953	United, 1967	
162	RHN763	163	RHN764	164	RHN765	165	RHN766	166	RHN767
200-204		Bristol SC4LK		Eastern Coach Works		B35F	1957-59		
200	UAO373	201	UAO374	202	VAO391	203	XAO610	204	XAO611

205	ONV428	Bristol SC4LK	Eastern Coach Works	B35F	1957	United Counties, 1963
206	ONV429	Bristol SC4LK	Eastern Coach Works	B35F	1957	United Counties, 1963
207	ONV430	Bristol SC4LK	Eastern Coach Works	B35F	1957	United Counties, 1963
208	OCY952	Bristol SC4LK	Eastern Coach Works	B35F	1957	United Welsh, 1963
209	605JPU	Bristol SC4LK	Eastern Coach Works	B35F	1958	Eastern National, 1964
210	606JPU	Bristol SC4LK	Eastern Coach Works	B35F	1958	Eastern National, 1964
211	607JPU	Bristol SC4LK	Eastern Coach Works	B35F	1958	Eastern National, 1964
224	NRM372	Bristol LS6G	Eastern Coach Works	C39F	1954	

Opposite, top:- **For rural routes many Tilling companies used the lightweight Bristol SC4LK, powered by a four-cylinder Gardner engine and fitted with a 35-seat ECW body. Cumberland ran 12.** *Reg Wilson*
Opposite, bottom:- **1966 saw the arrival of a pair of RELLs for Cumberland and these carried the rounded ECW bodywork. Shown in Keswick is newly delivered 261. The type replaced double-decks on the Penrith service.** *Bill Potter*

Cumberland operated two Bedford VALs with 51-seat Duple Vega Major bodies. One of the pair, 1301, is shown complete with headrest covers. *Bill Potter*

225-246   Bristol MW6G   Eastern Coach Works   B45F*   1960-66   *225-8 are DP41F

225	511BRM	230	426LAO	235	DAO207C	239	DAO211C	243	JAO243D
226	512BRM	231	AAO34B	236	DAO208C	240	DAO212C	244	JAO244D
227	119DRM	232	AAO35B	237	DAO209C	241	FRM617C	245	JAO245D
228	120DRM	233	DAO205C	238	DAO210C	242	JAO242D	246	JAO246D
229	425LAO	234	DAO206C						

250	JAO250D	Bristol RELL6G	Eastern Coach Works	B54F	1966
251	JAO251D	Bristol RELL6G	Eastern Coach Works	B54F	1966

252-276   Bristol RELL6L   Eastern Coach Works   B53F   1967-68

252	KRM252E	257	KRM257E	262	MRM262F	267	OAO267F	272	OAO272F
253	KRM253E	258	MRM258F	263	MRM263F	268	OAO268F	273	OAO273F
254	KRM260E	259	MRM259F	264	OAO264F	269	OAO269F	274	OAO274F
255	KRM261E	260	MRM260F	265	OAO265F	270	OAO270F	275	OAO275F
256	KRM262E	261	MRM261F	266	OAO266F	271	OAO271F	276	OAO276F

277	NRM374	Bristol LS6G	Eastern Coach Works	C39F	1954

372-389   Leyland Titan PD2/12   Leyland   L27/28R   1951

372	KRM254	378	KRM260	383	KRM265	385	KRM267	388	KRM270
374	KRM256	380	KRM262	384	KRM266	386	KRM268	389	KRM271
377	KRM259	381	KRM263						

390-399   Leyland Titan PD2/12   Leyland   L27/28R   1952

390	LRM102	392	LRM104	394	LRM106	396	LRM108	398	LRM110
391	LRM103	393	LRM105	395	LRM107	397	LRM109	399	LRM111

400-404

Bristol Lodekka LD6G Eastern Coach Works H33/25R 1954

400	ORM135	401	ORM136	402	ORM137	403	ORM138	404	ORM139

405-439

Bristol Lodekka LD6G Eastern Coach Works H33/27R 1954-59

405	ORM140	412	RAO729	419	UAO377	426	UAO384	433	XAO603
406	ORM141	413	RAO730	420	UAO378	427	UAO385	434	XAO604
407	ORM142	414	RAO731	421	UAO379	428	UAO386	435	XAO605
408	ORM143	415	RAO732	422	UAO380	429	VAO387	436	XAO606
409	ORM144	416	RAO733	423	UAO381	430	VAO388	437	XAO607
410	RAO727	417	UAO375	424	UAO382	431	VAO389	438	XAO608
411	RAO728	418	UAO376	425	UAO383	432	XAO602	439	XAO609

500-504

Bristol Lodekka FSF6B Eastern Coach Works H34/26F 1960

500	501BRM	501	502BRM	502	503BRM	503	504BRM	504	505BRM

505-521

Bristol Lodekka FLF6G Eastern Coach Works H38/32F 1961-64

505	506BRM	509	510BRM	513	117DRM	516	710GRM	519	713GRM
506	507BRM	510	114DRM	514	118DRM	517	711GRM	520	714GRM
507	508BRM	511	115DRM	515	709GRM	518	712GRM	521	AAO36B
508	509BRM	512	116DRM						

522	AAO37B	Bristol Lodekka FLF6B	Eastern Coach Works	H38/32F	1964
523	AAO38B	Bristol Lodekka FLF6B	Eastern Coach Works	H38/32F	1964
524	AAO39B	Bristol Lodekka FLF6B	Eastern Coach Works	H38/32F	1964

525-535

Bristol Lodekka FLF6G Eastern Coach Works H38/32F 1964-66

525	AAO575B	528	CRM472C	530	DAO202C	532	DAO204C	534	HRM534D
526	CAO649B	529	DAO201C	531	DAO203C	533	HRM533D	535	HRM535D
527	CRM211B								

550-554

Bristol Lodekka FS6G Eastern Coach Works H38/27R 1961

550	109DRM	551	110DRM	552	111DRM	553	112DRM	554	113DRM

555-565

Bristol Lodekka FS6B Eastern Coach Works H38/27R 1962-64

555	715GRM	558	718GRM	560	720GRM	562	421LAO	564	AAO574B
556	716GRM	559	719GRM	561	420LOA	563	AAO573B	565	BRM79B
557	717GRM								

1276-1282

Bristol LS6G Eastern Coach Works C39F 1954-56

1276	NRM373	1279	ORM134	1280	RAO734	1281	RAO735	1282	RAO736
1278	ORM133								

1283	VAO300	Bristol MW6G	Eastern Coach Works	C39F	1958
1284	XAO600	Bristol MW6G	Eastern Coach Works	C39F	1959
1285	XAO601	Bristol MW6G	Eastern Coach Works	C39F	1959
1300	FRM618C	Bedford VAL14	Duple Vega Major	C51F	1965
1301	GAO38D	Bedford VAL14	Duple Vega Major	C51F	1966
1302	LAO580E	Bedford VAL14	Duple Viceroy	C51F	1967
1302	LAO580E	Bedford VAL14	Duple Viceroy	C51F	1967

Livery: Tilling red and cream

DARWEN

Darwen Corporation Transport Department, Fisher Street, Darwen

Electric tramcars were introduced by Darwen Corporation in 1900, following the acquisition of the Blackburn and Over Darwen Steam Tramways Company's operations in 1898. The Corporation's first buses were four Leyland Lions in 1926 and small numbers of Lions were purchased over the following decade - there were 13 in operation in 1936. This was the year the last new trams were delivered, a pair of striking Brush streamliners. In the following year a start was made in abandoning the tramway operation and the last Darwen tram ran in October 1946. The replacements were generally Leyland Titans, starting in 1937 with four - the fleet's first double-deckers and its first diesels.

Postwar orders were divided between Leyland and Crossley - and included as late as 1957 four AECs which carried Crossley badging. Subsequent new buses were Leyland Titans.

The future: Darwen Corporation Transport vanished in 1974 when, as a result of local government reorganisation, the operation was absorbed by neighbouring Blackburn. The enlarged fleet adopted a new livery which incorporated both red and green, acknowledging the principal colours of its two constituent operators.

2	GTB163	Leyland Titan PD1	Leyland/Alexander	H30/26R	1946
3	GTB164	Leyland Titan PD1	Leyland/Alexander	H30/26R	1946
4	GTB165	Leyland Titan PD1	Leyland/Alexander	H30/26R	1946
8	GTC566	Leyland Titan PD1A	Leyland	H30/26R	1947
9	GTC567	Leyland Titan PD1A	Leyland	H30/26R	1947
10	OTD576	Leyland Titan PD2/10	Leyland	H30/26R	1952
11	OTD577	Leyland Titan PD2/10	Leyland	H30/26R	1953

It might look like an AEC badge on the front of this Reliance, but the famous triangle actually carries the name Crossley. Darwen operated three Crossley-badged Reliances with East Lancs bodies.
Bill Potter

In 1964 Darwen adopted the forward-entrance layout for double-deckers and quickly built up a fleet of PD3A and shorter PD2A Titans, all bodied by East Lancs. The PD3As seated 72, while the PD2As were 65-seaters.
Roy Marshall

12	RTJ609	Leyland Titan PD2/10	Leyland	H30/26R	1954	
13	RTJ610	Leyland Titan PD2/10	Leyland	H30/26R	1954	
14	WTB166	Leyland Titan PD2/22	Crossley	H30/26R	1955	
15	WTB167	Leyland Titan PD2/22	Crossley	H30/26R	1955	
16	WTB168	Leyland Titan PD2/22	East Lancashire	H30/26R	1955	
17	434BTE	Crossley Regent V D3RV	East Lancashire	H31/28R	1957	
18	435BTE	Crossley Reliance MU3RV	East Lancashire	B43F	1957	
19	436BTE	Crossley Reliance MU3RV	East Lancashire	B43F	1957	
20	739DTC	Crossley Reliance MU3RV	East Lancashire	B43F	1958	
22	TOU321	AEC Reliance 2MU3RV	Harrington	DP43F	1958	Parlane's Coaches, Aldershot, 1962
23	YTD290D	Leyland Tiger Cub PSUC1/13	East Lancashire	DP41F	1966	
24	461GTD	Leyland Titan PD2/31	East Lancashire	H31/28R	1959	
25	462GTD	Leyland Titan PD2/31	East Lancashire	H31/28R	1959	
26	463GTD	Leyland Titan PD2/31	East Lancashire	H31/28R	1959	
27	FTD249B	Leyland Titan PD3A/1	East Lancashire	H41/31F	1964	
28	FTD250B	Leyland Titan PD3A/1	East Lancashire	H41/31F	1964	
29	MTJ967C	Leyland Titan PD3A/1	East Lancashire	H41/31F	1965	
30	MTJ968C	Leyland Titan PD3A/1	East Lancashire	H41/31F	1965	
31	MTJ969C	Leyland Titan PD3A/1	East Lancashire	H41/31F	1965	
32	YTD287D	Leyland Titan PD2A/27	East Lancashire	H37/28F	1966	
33	YTD288D	Leyland Titan PD2A/27	East Lancashire	H37/28F	1966	
34	YTD289D	Leyland Titan PD2A/27	East Lancashire	H37/28F	1966	
35	KTD371	Crossley DD42/7	Crossley	H30/26R	1949	
36	ETF484F	Leyland Titan PD2A/27	East Lancashire	H37/28F	1967	
37	ETF485F	Leyland Titan PD2A/27	East Lancashire	H37/28F	1967	
38	ETF486F	Leyland Titan PD2A/27	East Lancashire	H37/28F	1967	
39	JTF217F	Leyland Titan PD2A/47	East Lancashire	H37/28F	1968	
40	JTF218F	Leyland Titan PD2A/47	East Lancashire	H37/28F	1968	
41	JTF219F	Leyland Titan PD2A/47	East Lancashire	H37/28F	1968	

On order: 3 Leyland Titan PD2A/27 /East Lancashire
Livery: Red and cream.

The 1968 North West Bus Handbook

HASLINGDEN

Haslingden Corporation Transport Department, John Street, Haslingden

Haslingden Corporation bought its first bus, a Leyland X, in 1906, for a service to Helmshore. This lasted until 1908. Bus operation recommenced in 1919, and expanded in 1930-31 with the purchase of eight Leyland Lions. Haslingden's first double-decker, a Titan, entered service in 1932. Throughout its entire history Haslingden owned just 50 buses, all but eight of which came from Leyland. Haslingden, Ramsbottom and Rawtenstall shared the same general manager in the 1960s - and bought similar types of bus.

The future: The Haslingden and Rawtenstall undertakings were merged to create a new Rossendale Joint Transport Committee on 1 April 1968. This was acquired by the newly-created Rossendale Borough Council in 1974 and became Rossendale Transport Ltd in 1986, remaining in local authority ownership and expanding its sphere of influence into Greater Manchester on tendered services.

Haslingden was one of the smallest municipal fleets in Lancashire, and was managed by the general manager of nearby Rawtenstall. Its fleet was made up primarily of Leyland Titans. The older examples had Leyland bodywork while this 1954 bus marked the switch to East Lancs who bodied all subsequent deliveries. *Reg Wilson*

The 1968 North West Bus Handbook

In 1966 Haslingden took delivery of its biggest bus yet and started the number series again. Number 1, is a 73-seat East Lancs-bodied PD3. A similar vehicle followed in 1967. *Roy Marshall*

1	XTF98D	Leyland Titan PD3/4	East Lancashire	H41/32F	1966	
2	DTJ960E	Leyland Titan PD3/14	East Lancashire	H41/32F	1967	
5	TTB302	Leyland Titan PD2/12	East Lancashire	H31/28R	1954	
6	MTC385	Leyland Titan PD2/1	Leyland	H30/26R	1950	
8	NTD530	Leyland Titan PD2/1	Leyland	H30/26R	1951	
9	OTF164	Leyland Titan PD2/12	Leyland	H30/26R	1953	
10	PTF207	Leyland Titan PD2/12	Leyland	H30/26R	1953	
11	PTF208	Leyland Titan PD2/12	Leyland	H30/26R	1953	
12	VTJ90	Leyland Titan PD2/12	East Lancashire	H31/28R	1955	
13	11CTB	Leyland Titan PD2/12	East Lancashire	H31/28R	1957	
14	192OTB	Leyland Titan PD2/41	East Lancashire	H31/28R	1960	
15	MTC256	Leyland Royal Tiger PSU1/13	Roe	B44F	1950	Ramsbottom, 1962
16	MTC257	Leyland Royal Tiger PSU1/13	Roe	B44F	1950	Ramsbottom, 1962
17	FTF732B	Leyland Leopard L1	East Lancashire	B44F	1964	
18	NTJ808C	Leyland Leopard L1	East Lancashire	B44F	1964	
	WTC763D	Morris J2BM	Morris	M11	1966	

Vehicles ordered by Haslingden and delivered during 1968 to Rossendale Transport which was formed 1st April 1968.

55	LTD955F	Leyland Leopard PSU4/2R	East Lancashire	B46F	1968
56	LTD956F	Leyland Leopard PSU4/2R	East Lancashire	B46F	1968

Livery:- Blue , cream and white

LANCASHIRE UNITED

Lancashire United Transport, Howe Bridge, Atherton

Lancashire United Tramways was registered in 1905 to take over the ailing South Lancashire Electric Traction and Power Co. Motorbus operation started in Leigh in 1906 but was soon abandoned. Another brief foray into bus operation was tried in 1914, then in 1919 came the start of serious bus operation with the purchase of 25 ex-War Department Dennises. Leyland double-deckers were introduced in 1925, and it was Leyland which supplied the bulk of the company's new buses until 1942.

The company's operating area extended from Liverpool to Manchester, and there was considerable joint working of services with the municipal operators in the area, and with Ribble.

In 1948 the company's name was changed to Lancashire United Transport. In the mid-1950s LUT buses replaced the trolleybuses of the associated South Lancashire Transport Co - that company was wound up when trolleybus operation came to an end in 1958.

LUT's postwar purchases saw Leyland relegated to a minority supplier, as the company added AECs, Atkinsons, Daimlers, Dennises, Fodens and Guys to its fleet. Guy Arab double-deckers dominated the fleet for much of the postwar period.

LUT was one of the biggest independent bus operators in Britain in the 1950s and 1960s.

The future: LUT was acquired by the Greater Manchester PTE in 1976, at which time the company ran 363 buses and coaches from three depots. The company retained its red and grey livery until 1978, when a variant of GMT's orange and white was applied. LUT was finally absorbed by GMT in 1981.

LUT was an early user of the Daimler Fleetline, although it would continue to buy Guy Arabs until 1967. Its first Fleetlines were six delivered in 1962 with lowheight Northern Counties bodies. Number 100 prepares to leave Bolton on the Manchester to Blackpool express service which was operated jointly with Ribble and North Western.
Roy Marshall

1-5
AEC Reliance 2MU3RV — Burlingham — DP41F — 1959

1	241GTJ	2	242GTJ	3	243GTJ	4	244GTJ	5	245GTJ

6	101JTD	Dennis Loline 6LW	Northern Counties	H40/29R	1959
7	102JTD	Dennis Loline 6LW	Northern Counties	H40/29R	1959

8-17
Daimler CSG6 — Northern Counties — H41/32R — 1959

8	103JTD	10	105JTD	12	107JTD	14	109JTD	16	111JTD
9	104JTD	11	106JTD	13	108JTD	15	110JTD	17	112JTD

18-27
Guy Arab IV 6LW — Northern Counties — H41/32R — 1959* — *27 is 6LX

18	113JTD	20	115JTD	22	117JTD	24	119JTD	26	121JTD
19	114JTD	21	116JTD	23	118JTD	25	120JTD	27	122JTD

28-35
Leyland Tiger Cub PSUC1/2 — Northern Counties — C41F — 1960

28	121MTE	30	123MTE	32	125MTE	34	127MTE	35	128MTE
29	122MTE	31	124MTE	33	126MTE				

36	826MTD	Dennis Loline 6LW	Northern Counties	H40/29R	1960
37	827MTD	Dennis Loline 6LW	Northern Counties	H40/29R	1960
38	828MTD	Dennis Loline 6LW	Northern Counties	H40/29R	1960
39	829MTD	Dennis Loline 6LW	Northern Counties	H40/29R	1960
40	531RTB	Guy Arab IV	Northern Counties (1965)	H41/32F	1960

41-49
Guy Arab IV — Metro-Cammell — H41/32R — 1961

41	532RTB	43	534RTB	45	536RTB	47	538RTB	49	540RTB
42	533RTB	44	535RTB	46	537RTB	48	539RTB		

50-60
Guy Arab IV — Northern Counties — H41/32R — 1960-61

50	141NTF	52	143NTF	54	145NTF	56	147NTF	59	565VTJ
51	142NTF	53	144NTF	55	146NTF	57	148NTF	60	566VTJ

61-80
Guy Arab IV — Northern Counties — H41/32R — 1961

61	501VTB	65	505VTB	69	509VTB	73	513VTB	77	517VTB
62	502VTB	66	506VTB	70	510VTB	74	514VTB	78	518VTB
63	503VTB	67	507VTB	71	511VTB	75	515VTB	79	519VTB
64	504VTB	68	508VTB	72	512VTB	76	516VTB	80	520VTB

81-96
AEC Reliance 2MU3RA — Plaxton Highway — DP41F — 1961-62

81	271STF	85	275STF	88	278STF	91	615WTE	94	618WTE
82	272STF	86	276STF	89	613WTE	92	616WTE	95	619WTE
83	273STF	87	277STF	90	614WTE	93	617WTE	96	620WTE
84	274STF								

97-102
Daimler Fleetline CRG6LX — Northern Counties — H43/33F — 1962

97	561TD	99	563TD	100	564TD	101	565TD	102	566TD
98	562TD								

103-119
Guy Arab IV — Northern Counties — H41/32R — 1962

103	567TD	107	571TD	111	575TD	114	578TD	117	581TD
104	568TD	108	572TD	112	576TD	115	579TD	118	582TD
105	569TD	109	573TD	113	577TD	116	580TD	119	583TD
106	570TD	110	574TD						

120-135
Guy Arab V — Northern Counties — H41/32R — 1963

120	6204TF	124	6208TF	127	6211TF	130	6214TF	133	6217TF
121	6205TF	125	6209TF	128	6212TF	131	6215TF	134	6218TF
122	6206TF	126	6210TF	129	6213TF	132	6216TF	135	6219TF
123	6207TF								

136	6220TF	Guy Arab V	Northern Counties	H41/32F	1963
137	8100TD	Daimler Fleetline CRG6LW	Northern Counties	H43/33F	1962

Seven Marshall-bodied Leyland Leopards were supplied in 1965 and, while these were similar to the BET product, those for LUT featured a rear view lower window which consumed the space for one seat. The effect is shown in this view of 206 pictured at Atherton. *Bill Potter*

138-142	Daimler Fleetline CRG6LX		Northern Counties		H43/31F	1963		
138	4611TF	139	4612TF	140	4613TF	141	4614TF	142	4615TF

| 143 | 8087TE | AEC Reliance 2U3RA | Plaxton Highway | B50F | 1963 |
| 144 | 8088TE | AEC Reliance 2U3RA | Plaxton Highway | B50F | 1963 |

145-150	AEC Reliance 2U3RA		Plaxton Highway		DP45F	1963		
145	8089TE	147	8091TE	148	8092TE	149	8093TE	150	8094TE
146	8090TE								

151-155	Leyland Leopard PSU3/3		Plaxton Highway		DP45F	1964		
151	DTF581B	152	DTF582B	153	DTF583B	154	DTF584B	155	DTF585B

156	DTF586B	Leyland Leopard PSU3/3	Plaxton Highway	B50F	1964
157	DTF587B	Leyland Leopard PSU3/3	Plaxton Highway	B50F	1964
158	DTF588B	Leyland Leopard PSU3/3	Plaxton Highway	B50F	1964

159-170	Guy Arab V		Northern Counties		H41/32F	1964-65		
159	KTC792C	162	KTC794C	165	HTJ521B	167	HTJ522B	169	HTJ524B
160	KTC793C	163	KTC795C	166	JTD300B	168	HTJ523B	170	HTJ525B
161	JTD299B	164	KTC791C						

Opposite, top:- 1964 saw the arrival of eight Plaxton Highway-bodied Leyland Leopards. The first five were to dual-purpose specification and were often found on the Blackpool service. The final three were to bus specification typified by 156, which carried stage carriage livery. *Bill Potter*
Opposite, bottom: Lancashire United provided links between Manchester and the towns to the west. The Guy Arab continued to find favour in the fleet and in 1966, when 218, entered service, a further 23 were added to the fleet. It is pictured leaving Salford Greengate on route 31. *Bill Potter*

The LUT coach livery switched from cream to grey with the delivery of a batch of Plaxton-bodied Leopards in 1965. These were short-wheelbase L2 models and were 43-seaters. *Reg Wilson*

171-185
Daimler Fleetline CRG6 · Northern Counties · H43/31F · 1964-65

171	ETD941B	174	ETD944B	177	ETD947B	180	ETD950B	183	PTE633C
172	ETD942B	175	ETD945B	178	ETD948B	181	PTE631C	184	PTE634C
173	ETD943B	176	ETD946B	179	ETD949B	182	PTE632C	185	PTE635C

186-195
Guy Arab V · Northern Counties · H41/32F · 1965

186	RTC351C	188	RTC353C	190	RTC355C	192	RTC357C	194	RTC359C
187	RTC352C	189	RTC354C	191	RTC356C	193	RTC358C	195	RTC360C

196-203
Leyland Leopard L2 · Plaxton Panorama · C43F · 1965

196	LTB305C	198	LTB307C	200	LTE265D	202	LTE267D	203	LTE268D
197	LTB306C	199	LTE264D	201	LTE266D				

204-210
Leyland Leopard PSU3/1 · Marshall · B50F* · 1965 · *205-208 are B46F

204	LTB301C	206	LTB303C	208	LTE261C	209	LTE262C	210	LTE263C
205	LTB302C	207	LTB304C						

211	TTF175D	Leyland Tiger Cub PSUC1/11	Willowbrook	B44F	1966
212	TTF176D	Leyland Tiger Cub PSUC1/11	Willowbrook	B44F	1966
213	TTF177D	Leyland Tiger Cub PSUC1/11	Willowbrook	B44F	1966
214	UTC766D	Leyland Leopard L2	Plaxton Panorama	C43F	1966
215	UTC767D	Leyland Leopard L2	Plaxton Panorama	C43F	1966
216	UTC768D	Leyland Leopard L2	Plaxton Panorama	C43F	1966
217	UTC769D	Leyland Leopard L2	Plaxton Panorama	C43F	1966

The 1968 North West Bus Handbook

LUT often pursued an individualistic approach to single-deckers. In 1967 it took the unusual combination of Bristol RE chassis and Plaxton bodywork. Plaxton was the key supplier of single-deck bodies to the company. *Roy Marshall*

218-240 — Guy Arab V, Northern Counties, H41/32F, 1966

218	WTE141D	223	WTE146D	228	WTE151D	233	WTE156D	237	WTE160D
219	WTE142D	224	WTE147D	229	WTE152D	234	WTE157D	238	WTE161D
220	WTE143D	225	WTE148D	230	WTE153D	235	WTE158D	239	WTE162D
221	WTE144D	226	WTE149D	231	WTE154D	236	WTE159D	240	WTE163D
222	WTE145D	227	WTE150D	232	WTE155D				

241	YTC249D	Leyland Tiger Cub PSUC1/	Northen Counties	B40D	1966
242	ETJ125F	Leyland Tiger Cub PSUC1/	Marshall	B40D	1967
243	ETJ126F	Leyland Tiger Cub PSUC1/	Marshall	B40D	1967
244	ETJ127F	Leyland Tiger Cub PSUC1/	Marshall	B40D	1967

245-264 — Bristol RESL6G, Plaxton, B42D, 1967

245	CTE471E	249	CTE475E	253	CTE479E	257	CTE483E	261	CTE487E
246	CTE472E	250	CTE476E	254	CTE480E	258	CTE484E	262	CTE488E
247	CTE473E	251	CTE477E	255	CTE481E	259	CTE485E	263	CTE489E
248	CTE474E	252	CTE478E	256	CTE482E	260	CTE486E	264	CTE490E

265-290 — Guy Arab V, Northern Counties, H41/32F, 1967

265	ETJ901F	271	ETJ907F	276	ETJ912F	281	ETJ917F	286	ETJ922F
266	ETJ902F	272	ETJ908F	277	ETJ913F	282	ETJ918F	287	ETJ923F
267	ETJ903F	273	ETJ909F	278	ETJ914F	283	ETJ919F	288	ETJ924F
268	ETJ904F	274	ETJ910F	279	ETJ915F	284	ETJ920F	289	ETJ925F
269	ETJ905F	275	ETJ911F	280	ETJ916F	285	ETJ921F	290	ETJ926F
270	ETJ906F								

291	NTC108G	AEC Swift MP2R	Alexander W	B43D	1968
292	NTC109G	AEC Swift MP2R	Alexander W	B43D	1968
293	NTC110G	AEC Swift MP2R	Alexander W	B43D	1968

294-312 Bristol RESL6G Alexander W B42D On order for 1968-69

294	NTC111G	298	NTC115G	302	NTC119G	306	NTC123G	310	NTC127G
295	NTC112G	299	NTC116G	303	NTC120G	307	NTC124G	311	NTC128G
296	NTC113G	300	NTC117G	304	NTC121G	308	NTC125G	312	NTC129G
297	NTC114G	301	NTC118G	305	NTC122G	309	NTC126G		

516-521 Guy Arab UF Weymann DP40F 1954

516	STF201	518	STF203	519	STF204	520	STF205	521	STF206
517	STF202								

522-530 Atkinson Alpha PM745H Roe B44F 1954

522	TTD291	524	TTD293	526	TTD295	528	TTD297	530	TTD299
523	TTD292	525	TTD294	527	TTD296	529	TTD298		

531	TTD300	Atkinson Alpha PM745H	Northen Counties	B34C	1954

542-551 Guy Arab IV Northern Counties H33/28R 1955

542	WTB41	544	WTB43	546	WTB45	548	WTB47	550	WTB49
543	WTB42	545	WTB44	547	WTB46	549	WTB48	551	WTB50

552-561 Atkinson Alpha PL745H Roe DP40F 1955

552	WTB61	554	WTB63	556	WTB65	558	WTB67	560	WTB69
553	WTB62	555	WTB64	557	WTB66	559	WTB68	561	WTB70

562	WTB71	Leyland Tiger Cub PSUC1/1	Weymann	B44F	1956
563	WTB72	Leyland Tiger Cub PSUC1/1	Weymann	B44F	1956
564	FTC205	Guy Arab I	Northern Counties (1955)	H33/28R	1942
565	FTC207	Guy Arab I	Northern Counties (1955)	H33/28R	1942
566	FTC208	Guy Arab I	Northern Counties (1955)	H33/28R	1942
567	FTC210	Guy Arab I	Northern Counties (1955)	H33/28R	1942
568	FTE33	Guy Arab II	Northern Counties (1955)	H33/28R	1944
569	FTE39	Guy Arab II	Northern Counties (1955)	H33/28R	1944

Lancashire United Transport was one of Britain's biggest independents with an extensive network of services in the area between Liverpool and Manchester, many of which were worked jointly with other operators. Guys featured prominently in its fleet, with 603, a 1956 Arab IV, being the company's first 30ft-long double-decker. Northern Counties built the body on this - and on most other LUT double-deckers. *Roy Marshall*

The 1968 North West Bus Handbook

570-593 — Daimler CVG5K — Weymann — H33/28R — 1956

570	YTD871	575	YTD876	580	YTD881	585	YTD886	590	YTD891
571	YTD872	576	YTD877	581	YTD882	586	YTD887	591	YTD892
572	YTD873	577	YTD878	582	YTD883	587	YTD888	592	YTD893
573	YTD874	578	YTD879	583	YTD884	588	YTD889	593	YTD894
574	YTD875	579	YTD880	584	YTD885	589	YTD890		

594-602 — Guy Arab IV — Northern Counties — H36/28R — 1957

594	311ATC	596	313ATC	598	315ATC	600	317ATC	602	319ATC
595	312ATC	597	314ATC	599	316ATC	601	318ATC		

603-619 — Guy Arab IV — Northern Counties — H41/32R — 1956-58

603	320ATC	607	874DTB	611	878DTB	614	881DTB	617	884DTB
604	871DTB	608	875DTB	612	879DTB	615	882DTB	618	885DTB
605	872DTB	609	876DTB	613	880DTB	616	883DTB	619	886DTB
606	873DTB	610	877DTB						

620-629 — Leyland Tiger Cub PSUC1/2 — Duple — DP41F — 1957-58

620	951BTF	622	953BTF	624	955BTF	626	432DTF	628	434DTF
621	952BTF	623	954BTF	625	431DTF	627	433DTF	629	435DTF

630-643 — Guy Arab IV — Northern Counties — H41/32R — 1958

630	347FTB	633	350FTB	636	353FTB	639	356FTB	642	359FTB
631	348FTB	634	351FTB	637	354FTB	640	357FTB	643	360FTB
632	349FTB	635	352FTB	638	355FTB	641	358FTB		

644-657 — Leyland Titan PD3/4 — Metro-Cammell — H41/32R — 1958

644	561FTF	647	564FTF	650	567FTF	653	570FTF	656	573FTF
645	562FTF	648	565FTF	651	568FTF	654	571FTF	657	574FTF
646	563FTF	649	566FTF	652	569FTF	655	572FTF		

Livery: Red and cream

There were a few front-engined Daimlers in the LUT fleet, the last being eight CSG6/30 with manual gearboxes and Northern Counties bodies in 1959. Behind stands one of two Dennis Lolines delivered at the same time.
Geoff Lumb

The 1968 North West Bus Handbook

LANCASTER

Lancaster City Transport, Kingsway, Skerton, Lancaster

Operation of electric trams was started by Lancaster Corporation in 1903 and continued until 1930. The undertaking's first buses, in 1916, were battery-powered and these - five in total - lasted until 1929. Motorbus operation started in 1925. Most pre-war buses were Daimlers, although the first double-decker, in 1932, was an AEC Regent.

After the war a variety of makes joined the fleet - Crossley, Daimler and Leyland, as well as a few ex-London Transport Guys. From the late 1950s one-man-operation was a feature of some services, and to advance this Lancaster acquired four AEC Regal IVs from Rochdale, as well as converting existing single-deckers in the fleet.

The future: An enlarged Lancaster City Transport took over the neighbouring Morecambe & Heysham business when local government was reorganised in 1974 and adopted a new blue livery. It was reformed as a limited company in 1986, still owned by the council. The operation came to an end in 1993 when the council announced that it intended to sell the business. Prospective buyers were dissuaded from pursuing its purchase when Stagecoach Ribble registered new services over most of LCT's routes. Some of the company's assets were taken over by Stagecoach when it closed in August 1993.

70	FTD70	Daimler CWG5	Crossley (1950)	H30/26R	1943
101	101UTF	Leyland Leopard L1	East Lancashire	B42D	1961
102	102UTF	Leyland Leopard L1	East Lancashire	B42D	1961
103	103UTF	Leyland Leopard L1	East Lancashire	B42D	1961

Opposite: **The only half-cab single-decker in the Lancaster fleet, and one of just a handful still running in the north-west, was this 1952 Daimler CVG5 with Northern Counties body. It was retained primarily for use on a prison contract which required a compact vehicle. The Leyland Titans was the most numerous type in the Lancaster fleet, with 13 in use. From 1957 all new buses for Lancaster were bodied by East Lancs.**
Bill Potter/ Reg Wilson

Four East Lancashire-bodied Leyland Titan PD2s were placed in service with Lancaster during 1957, the first double-decks for the fleet from the Blackburn-based coachbuilder.
Roy Marshall

One-man-operated single-deckers played a small part in Lancaster's operations prior to the concept becoming more widespread in the second half of the 1960s. There were already Tiger Cubs and Leopards in service when six Panthers with East Lancs bodies joined the fleet in 1967-68. *Roy Marshall*

104	GTC104F	Leyland Panther PSUR1/1R	East Lancashire	B53F	1967	
105	GTC105F	Leyland Panther PSUR1/1R	East Lancashire	B53F	1967	
106	GTC106F	Leyland Panther PSUR1/1R	East Lancashire	B53F	1967	
107	LTC107F	Leyland Panther PSUR1/1R	East Lancashire	B53F	1968	
108	LTC108F	Leyland Panther PSUR1/1R	East Lancashire	B53F	1968	
109	LTC109F	Leyland Panther PSUR1/1R	East Lancashire	B53F	1968	
128	128DTD	Leyland Titan PD2/41	East Lancashire	H35/28R	1957	
129	129DTD	Leyland Titan PD2/41	East Lancashire	H35/28R	1957	
175	175FTJ	Leyland Tiger Cub PSUC1/3	East Lancashire	B43F	1958	
176	176FTJ	Leyland Tiger Cub PSUC1/3	East Lancashire	B43F	1958	
177	177FTJ	Leyland Tiger Cub PSUC1/3	East Lancashire	B43F	1958	
182	FTE182	Guy Arab II 5LW	Crossley (1950)	H30/26R	1944	

201-206

		Leyland Titan PD2/37	East Lancashire	H37/28F	1963-65

201	201YTE	203	203YTE	204	KTJ204C	205	KTJ205C	206	KTJ206C
202	202YTE								

389	389JTD	Leyland Tiger Cub PSUC1/3	East Lancashire	B43F	1959	
390	390JTD	Leyland Tiger Cub PSUC1/3	East Lancashire	B43F	1959	
466	NTF466	Daimler CVG5	Northern Counties	B32F	1952	
571	HTF571	Crossley DD42/3	Crossley	H30/26R	1947	
572	HTF572	Crossley DD42/3	Crossley	H30/26R	1947	
582	KTF582	AEC Regal III 9621E	Strachan	B36F	1949	Morecambe & Heysham, 1952
708	NTC708	Leyland Titan PD2/10	Leyland	H33/26R	1951	
709	NTC709	Leyland Titan PD2/10	Leyland	H33/26R	1951	
710	NTC710	Leyland Titan PD2/10	Leyland	H33/26R	1951	
711	JDK711	AEC Regal IV 9822E	Burlingham	B44F	1953	Rochdale Corporation, 1957
713	JDK713	AEC Regal IV 9822E	Burlingham	B44F	1953	Rochdale Corporation, 1957
714	JDK714	AEC Regal IV 9822E	Burlingham	B44F	1953	Rochdale Corporation, 1957
715	JDK715	AEC Regal IV 9822E	Burlingham	B44F	1953	Rochdale Corporation, 1957
726	FTD726	Guy Arab II 5LW	Guy/Park Royal(1952)	H30/26R	1943	
727	FTD727	Guy Arab II 5LW	Guy/Park Royal(1952)	H30/26R	1943	
881	881BTF	Leyland Titan PD2/41	East Lancashire	H35/28R	1957	
882	882BTF	Leyland Titan PD2/41	East Lancashire	H35/28R	1957	
961	JTD961	Crossley DD42/3	Crossley	H30/26R	1948	

Livery: Maroon and ivory.

The 1968 North West Bus Handbook

LEIGH

Leigh Corporation Transport, Holden Road, Leigh

Leigh Corporation never operated trams, and only started running buses after World War I, with the purchase six Straker Squires in 1920. Services expanded rapidly, and by the end of the decade Leigh was running 30 buses, including three Leyland Titan double-deckers. Leylands figured strongly in the Leigh fleet over the years.

Low bridges (and a low depot roof) meant that all double-deckers were of side-gangway lowbridge layout until the purchase of Dennis Lolines in 1958. The last lowbridge buses were two Titans in 1962; all subsequent double-deckers were AEC Renowns.

The fleet numbering system requires some explanation. It started at 1 in 1920, reaching 99 in 1943. At this point the lowest-numbered bus in the fleet was 40, and new buses from 1946 were numbered from 39 downwards. When this series got down to 4, subsequent new buses were numbered upwards from 40 to 65. From 1962 new buses were given numbers which filled gaps left by withdrawn vehicles.

The future: Leigh Corporation Transport was absorbed by the SELNEC PTE in November 1969.

1	187LTB	Leyland Tiger Cub PSUC1/2	East Lancashire	DP43F	1960
2	188LTB	Leyland Tiger Cub PSUC1/2	East Lancashire	DP43F	1960
3	778YTB	Leyland Titan PD3A/1	East Lancashire	L34/32R	1962
5	ATB246D	AEC Renown 3B3RA	East Lancashire	H41/31R	1966
7	KTD759	Leyland Titan PD2/1	Lydney	L27/26R	1949
8	HTJ761B	AEC Renown 3B3RA	East Lancashire	H41/31F	1964
10	KTD762	Leyland Titan PD2/1	Lydney	L27/26R	1949
11	PTC112C	AEC Renown 3B3RA	East Lancashire	H41/31F	1965

For a short period Leigh bought Dennis Lolines with East Lancashire bodies and Gardner engines. It had six, the newest being two Loline IIIs delivered in 1961. From 1963 Leigh switched to the AEC Renown, two of which can be seen in the background.
Roy Marshall

12	KTD764	Leyland Titan PD2/1	Lydney	L27/26R	1949	
13	PTC113C	AEC Renown 3B3RA	East Lancashire	H41/31F	1965	
14	KTD766	Leyland Titan PD2/1	Lydney	L27/26R	1949	
15	PTC114C	AEC Renown 3B3RA	East Lancashire	H41/31F	1965	
16	KTD768	Leyland Titan PD2/1	Lydney	L27/26R	1949	
17	KTD769	Leyland Titan PD2/1	Lydney	L27/26R	1949	
18	KTD770	Leyland Titan PD2/1	Lydney	L27/26R	1949	

20-24
Leyland Leopard PSU4/2R — East Lancashire — B45F — 1968

20	HTJ131F	21	HTJ132F	22	HTJ133F	23	HTJ134F	24	HTJ135F

21	JTB806	Leyland Titan PD2/1	Roberts	L27/26R	1948	
23	JTB804	Leyland Titan PD2/1	Roberts	L27/26R	1948	
24	JTB803	Leyland Titan PD2/1	Roberts	L27/26R	1948	
25	1972TJ	AEC Renown 3B3RA	East Lancashire	H41/31R	1963	
26	1973TJ	AEC Renown 3B3RA	East Lancashire	H41/31R	1963	
27	1974TJ	AEC Renown 3B3RA	East Lancashire	H41/31R	1963	
28	1975TJ	AEC Renown 3B3RA	East Lancashire	H41/31R	1963	
29	ATE190E	AEC Renown 3B3RA	East Lancashire	H41/31F	1967	
30	HTJ762B	AEC Renown 3B3RA	East Lancashire	H41/31F	1964	
31	YTJ627D	AEC Renown 3B3RA	East Lancashire	H41/31F	1966	
32	YTJ628D	AEC Renown 3B3RA	East Lancashire	H41/31F	1966	
34	HTJ763B	AEC Renown 3B3RA	East Lancashire	H41/31F	1964	
35	PTC115C	AEC Renown 3B3RA	East Lancashire	H41/31F	1965	
36	ATB245D	AEC Renown 3B3RA	East Lancashire	H41/31F	1966	
37	779YTB	Leyland Titan PD3A/1	East Lancashire	L34/32R	1962	
38	HTD328B	AEC Renown 3B3RA	East Lancashire	H41/31F	1964	
39	HTJ764B	AEC Renown 3B3RA	East Lancashire	H41/31F	1964	

40-46
AEC Regent III 9613E — East Lancashire — L27/26R — 1952

40	NTE381	42	NTE383	44	NTE385	45	NTE386	46	NTE387
41	NTE382	43	NTE384						

47-54
Leland Titan PD2/20 — East Lancashire — L30/28R — 1955-57

47	WTE21	49	WTE23	51	WTE25	53	723ATE	54	724ATE
48	WTE22	50	WTE24	52	722ATE				

55-59
Leland Titan PD2/30 — East Lancashire — L30/28R — 1957-58

55	491DTC	56	492DTC	57	493DTC	58	494DTC	59	495DTC

60	223FTC	Dennis Loline I 6LW	East Lancashire	H41/31R	1958	
61	224FTC	Dennis Loline I 6LW	East Lancashire	H41/31R	1958	
62	878GTF	Dennis Loline I 6LW	East Lancashire	H41/31R	1959	
63	879GTF	Dennis Loline I 6LW	East Lancashire	H41/31R	1959	
64	267WTE	Dennis Loline III 6LX	East Lancashire	H41/31R	1961	
65	268WTE	Dennis Loline III 6LX	East Lancashire	H41/31R	1961	

Livery:- Blue and cream

Opposite: **The swooping livery and conservatively-styled East Lancs body make this 1960 Leyland Tiger Cub operated by Leigh Corporation look rather older than it actually is. It was one of a pair. AEC Renowns with East Lancs bodywork were the Leigh standard for most of the 1960s. Five were delivered in 1964.** *Reg Wilson*

A type on its way out in 1968 was a combination unique in the north-west to Leigh Corporation - the Lydney-bodied Leyland Titan PD2. Of 12 delivered in 1949, seven remained in service. *Roy Marshall*

LIVERPOOL

Liverpool Corporation Transport, Edge Lane, Liverpool

Liverpool Corporation took over the Liverpool United Tramways and Omnibus Co in 1897. Electric trams started running the following year. In 1911 four motorbuses were acquired with the business of the Woolton Omnibus Co. A small number of buses - including one steam-powered Clarkson - were bought prior to the outbreak of the Great War.

Liverpool extended its tramways after the war and built new cars right through the 1930s. Consequently buses played a relatively small part in the Corporation's transport operations. In 1938, for example, it was running almost 750 trams but fewer than 120 buses, most of which were AEC Regents less than three years old. To cater for wartime workers Liverpool purchased over 80 Leyland double-deckers which had previously been owned by London Transport.

After the war more AECs were delivered, and a ten-year programme of replacing trams by buses was started. The last tram ran in 1957. Postwar bus orders were focused on AEC and Leyland, but there were Crossleys and Daimlers too. Until 1959 many had bodywork assembled at the Corporation's Edge Lane works.

Liverpool was one of the first big municipal operations to show whole-hearted commitment to the rear-engined double-decker, with an initial order for 200 Leyland Atlanteans which was announced in 1962. These had distinctively-styled Metro-Cammell bodywork. They were joined in 1968 by Panthers with Metro-Cammell bodies as the Corporation looked to large-scale one-man-operation to help reduce costs and ease staff shortages.

The future: Liverpool's bus fleet became the major constituent of the new Merseyside PTE on 1 December 1969.

A1-A38		AEC Regent III 9613S		Crossley			H30/26R	1953		
A1	NKD501	**A9**	NKD509	**A17**	NKD517	**A24**	NKD524	**A31**	NKD531
A2	NKD502	**A10**	NKD510	**A18**	NKD518	**A25**	NKD525	**A32**	NKD532
A3	NKD503	**A11**	NKD511	**A19**	NKD519	**A26**	NKD526	**A34**	NKD534
A4	NKD504	**A12**	NKD512	**A20**	NKD520	**A27**	NKD527	**A35**	NKD535
A5	NKD505	**A13**	NKD513	**A21**	NKD521	**A28**	NKD528	**A36**	NKD536
A6	NKD506	**A14**	NKD514	**A22**	NKD522	**A29**	NKD529	**A37**	NKD537
A7	NKD507	**A15**	NKD515	**A23**	NKD523	**A30**	NKD530	**A38**	NKD538
A8	NKD508	**A16**	NKD516						
A39	NKD539	AEC Regent III 9613S		Saro			H32/26R	1954		
A40	NKD540	AEC Regent III 9613S		Saro			H32/26R	1954		

Liverpool Corporation divided their chassis orders between AEC and Leyland, each with fleet letter identities. Seen heading for Seaforth docks is one of the Weymann body shells to be completed by Davidson.
Roy Marshall

A41-A100 AEC Regent III 9613S Crossley/LCPT H30/26R 1954-55

A41	NKD541	A53	NKD553	A66	NKD566	A78	NKD578	A90	NKD590
A42	NKD542	A54	NKD554	A67	NKD567	A79	NKD579	A91	NKD591
A43	NKD543	A55	NKD555	A68	NKD568	A80	NKD580	A92	NKD592
A44	NKD544	A56	NKD556	A69	NKD569	A81	NKD581	A93	NKD593
A45	NKD545	A57	NKD557	A70	NKD570	A82	NKD582	A94	NKD594
A46	NKD546	A58	NKD558	A71	NKD571	A83	NKD583	A95	NKD595
A47	NKD547	A60	NKD560	A72	NKD572	A84	NKD584	A96	NKD596
A48	NKD548	A61	NKD561	A73	NKD573	A85	NKD585	A97	NKD597
A49	NKD549	A62	NKD562	A74	NKD574	A86	NKD586	A98	NKD598
A50	NKD550	A63	NKD563	A75	NKD575	A87	NKD587	A99	NKD599
A51	NKD551	A64	NKD564	A76	NKD576	A88	NKD588	A100	NKD600
A52	NKD552	A65	NKD565	A77	NKD577	A89	NKD589		

A101-A127 AEC Regent V D3RV Crossley H32/26R 1955-56

A101	SKB101	A107	SKB107	A113	SKB113	A118	SKB118	A123	SKB123
A102	SKB102	A108	SKB108	A114	SKB114	A119	SKB119	A124	SKB124
A103	SKB103	A109	SKB109	A115	SKB115	A120	SKB120	A125	SKB125
A104	SKB104	A110	SKB110	A116	SKB116	A121	SKB121	A126	SKB126
A105	SKB105	A111	SKB111	A117	SKB117	A122	SKB122	A127	SKB127
A106	SKB106	A112	SKB112						

A128-A167 AEC Regent V D3RV Crossley/LCPT H32/26R 1955-56

A128	SKB128	A136	SKB136	A144	SKB144	A152	SKB152	A161	SKB161
A129	SKB129	A137	SKB137	A145	SKB145	A153	SKB153	A162	SKB162
A130	SKB130	A138	SKB138	A146	SKB146	A154	SKB154	A163	SKB163
A131	SKB131	A139	SKB139	A147	SKB147	A156	SKB156	A164	SKB164
A132	SKB132	A140	SKB140	A148	SKB148	A157	SKB157	A165	SKB165
A133	SKB133	A141	SKB141	A149	SKB149	A158	SKB158	A166	SKB166
A134	SKB134	A142	SKB142	A150	SKB150	A159	SKB159	A167	SKB167
A135	SKB135	A143	SKB143	A151	SKB151	A160	SKB160		

A168-A202   AEC Regent V D3RV   Metro-Cammell Orion   H33/29R   1956-57

A168	VKB766	A175	VKB773	A182	VKB780	A189	VKB787	A196	VKB794
A169	VKB767	A176	VKB774	A183	VKB781	A190	VKB788	A197	VKB795
A170	VKB768	A177	VKB775	A184	VKB782	A191	VKB789	A198	VKB796
A171	VKB769	A178	VKB776	A185	VKB783	A192	VKB790	A199	VKB797
A172	VKB770	A179	VKB777	A186	VKB784	A193	VKB791	A200	VKB798
A173	VKB771	A180	VKB778	A187	VKB785	A194	VKB792	A201	VKB799
A174	VKB772	A181	VKB779	A188	VKB786	A195	VKB793	A202	VKB800

A203-A232   AEC Regent V D3RV   Metro-Cammell/LCPT   H33/29R   1957-58

A203	VKB801	A209	VKB807	A215	VKB813	A221	VKB819	A227	VKB825
A204	VKB802	A210	VKB808	A216	VKB814	A222	VKB820	A228	VKB826
A205	VKB803	A211	VKB809	A217	VKB815	A223	VKB821	A229	VKB827
A206	VKB804	A212	VKB810	A218	VKB816	A224	VKB822	A220	VKB828
A207	VKB805	A213	VKB811	A219	VKB817	A225	VKB823	A231	VKB829
A208	VKB806	A214	VKB812	A220	VKB818	A226	VKB824	A232	VKB830

A233-A292   AEC Regent V D3RV   Metro-Cammell   H33/29R   1957-58

A233	VKB866	A245	VKB878	A257	VKB890	A269	WKF227	A281	WKF239
A234	VKB867	A246	VKB879	A258	VKB891	A270	WKF228	A282	WKF240
A235	VKB868	A247	VKB880	A259	VKB892	A271	WKF229	A283	WKF241
A236	VKB869	A248	VKB881	A260	VKB893	A272	WKF230	A284	WKF242
A237	VKB870	A249	VKB882	A261	VKB894	A273	WKF231	A285	WKF243
A238	VKB871	A250	VKB883	A262	VKB895	A274	WKF232	A286	WKF244
A239	VKB872	A251	VKB884	A263	VKB896	A275	WKF233	A287	WKF245
A240	VKB873	A252	VKB885	A264	VKB897	A276	WKF234	A288	WKF246
A241	VKB874	A253	VKB886	A265	VKB898	A277	WKF235	A289	WKF247
A242	VKB875	A254	VKB887	A266	VKB899	A278	WKF236	A290	WKF248
A243	VKB876	A255	VKB888	A267	VKB900	A279	WKF237	A291	WKF249
A244	VKB877	A256	VKB889	A268	WKF226	A280	WKF238	A292	WKF250

A659	JKF902	AEC Regent III 9612E	Weymann/LCPT	H30/26R	1949
A662	JKF905	AEC Regent III 9612E	Weymann/LCPT	H30/26R	1949
A664	JKF907	AEC Regent III 9612E	Weymann/LCPT	H30/26R	1950
A673	JKF916	AEC Regent III 9612E	Weymann/LCPT	H30/26R	1949
A686	JKF929	AEC Regent III 9612E	Weymann/Davidson	H30/26R	1951
A695	JKF938	AEC Regent III 9612E	Weymann/Davidson	H30/26R	1951
A715	JKF958	AEC Regent III 9612E	Weymann/Blakes	H30/26R	1951
A716	JKF959	AEC Regent III 9612E	Weymann/Blakes	H30/26R	1951
A717	JKF960	AEC Regent III 9612E	Weymann/Aero Engineering	H30/26R	1951
A724	JKF967	AEC Regent III 9612E	Weymann/Blakes	H30/26R	1951
A725	JKF968	AEC Regent III 9612E	Weymann/Blakes	H30/26R	1951
A726	JKF969	AEC Regent III 9612E	Weymann/Pearson	H30/26R	1951
A728	JKF971	AEC Regent III 9612E	Weymann/Blakes	H30/26R	1951
A730	JKF973	AEC Regent III 9612E	Weymann/Blakes	H30/26R	1951
A732	JKF975	AEC Regent III 9612E	Weymann/Aero Engineering	H30/26R	1950
A733	JKF976	AEC Regent III 9612E	Weymann/Pearson	H30/26R	1951
A740	JKF983	AEC Regent III 9612E	Weymann/Davidson	H30/26R	1951
A744	JKF987	AEC Regent III 9612E	Weymann/Aero Engineering	H30/26R	1950
A747	JKF990	AEC Regent III 9612E	Weymann/Aero Engineering	H30/26R	1951
A751	JKF994	AEC Regent III 9612E	Weymann/Blakes	H30/26R	1951
A752	JKF995	AEC Regent III 9612E	Weymann/Blakes	H30/26R	1951
A755	JKF998	AEC Regent III 9612E	Weymann/Blakes	H30/26R	1951

A757-A806   AEC Regent III 9613A   Crossley   H30/26R   1951-52

A757	MKB950	A767	MKB960	A777	MKB970	A788	MKB981	A797	MKB990
A758	MKB951	A768	MKB961	A778	MKB971	A789	MKB982	A799	MKB992
A759	MKB952	A770	MKB963	A779	MKB972	A790	MKB983	A800	MKB993
A760	MKB953	A771	MKB964	A781	MKB974	A791	MKB984	A801	MKB994
A761	MKB954	A772	MKB965	A782	MKB975	A792	MKB985	A802	MKB995
A762	MKB955	A773	MKB966	A783	MKB976	A793	MKB986	A803	MKB996
A764	MKB957	A774	MKB967	A784	MKB977	A794	MKB987	A804	MKB997
A765	MKB958	A775	MKB968	A785	MKB978	A795	MKB988	A805	MKB998
A766	MKB959	A776	MKB969	A786	MKB979	A796	MKB989	A806	MKB999

Liverpool's last AEC Regent was also the undertaking's only forward-entrance front-engined double-decker. One of three experimental buses, E1, was to give way to Atlantean E2 as the prototype for future deliveries. It had Park Royal bodywork similar to that being built for East Kent. *Stewart J Brown*

E1	371BKA	AEC Regent V LD2RA	Park Royal	FH40/32F	1959	
E2	372BKA	Leyland Atlantean PDR1/1	Metro-Cammell	H44/34F	1959	
E3	116TMD	AEC Bridgemaster B3RA	Park Royal	H45/31R	1958	AEC demonstrator, 1959

L1-L60

Leyland Titan PD2/12 — Weymann Aurora — H32/26R — 1953

L1	NKD601	**L13**	NKD613	**L26**	NKD626	**L39**	NKD639	**L50**	NKD650
L2	NKD602	**L15**	NKD615	**L28**	NKD628	**L40**	NKD640	**L51**	NKD651
L3	NKD603	**L16**	NKD616	**L29**	NKD629	**L41**	NKD641	**L52**	NKD652
L4	NKD604	**L17**	NKD617	**L30**	NKD630	**L42**	NKD642	**L53**	NKD653
L5	NKD605	**L18**	NKD618	**L31**	NKD631	**L43**	NKD643	**L54**	NKD654
L6	NKD606	**L19**	NKD619	**L32**	NKD632	**L44**	NKD644	**L55**	NKD655
L7	NKD607	**L20**	NKD620	**L33**	NKD633	**L45**	NKD645	**L56**	NKD656
L8	NKD608	**L21**	NKD621	**L34**	NKD634	**L46**	NKD646	**L57**	NKD657
L9	NKD609	**L22**	NKD622	**L35**	NKD635	**L47**	NKD647	**L58**	NKD658
L10	NKD610	**L23**	NKD623	**L36**	NKD636	**L48**	NKD648	**L59**	NKD659
L11	NKD611	**L24**	NKD624	**L37**	NKD637	**L49**	NKD649	**L60**	NKD660
L12	NKD612	**L25**	NKD625	**L38**	NKD638				

L61-L90

Leyland Titan PD2/20 — Alexander — H30/26R — 1954

L61	NKD661	**L67**	NKD667	**L73**	NKD673	**L79**	NKD679	**L85**	NKD685
L62	NKD662	**L68**	NKD668	**L74**	NKD674	**L80**	NKD680	**L86**	NKD686
L63	NKD663	**L69**	NKD669	**L75**	NKD675	**L81**	NKD681	**L87**	NKD687
L64	NKD664	**L70**	NKD670	**L76**	NKD676	**L82**	NKD682	**L88**	NKD688
L65	NKD665	**L71**	NKD671	**L77**	NKD677	**L83**	NKD683	**L89**	NKD689
L66	NKD666	**L72**	NKD672	**L78**	NKD678	**L84**	NKD684	**L90**	NKD690

The use of cream surrounds for the main side windows was an unusual feature of Liverpool's livery in the late 1960s, at a time when most fleets extended the relief colour around the front and rear of the bodywork. Weymann built the body on L19, a 1953 PD2. *Roy Marshall*

L91-L140 Leyland Titan PD2/20 Duple H32/26R 1954-55

L91	RKC192	L101	RKC202	L111	RKC212	L121	RKC222	L131	RKC232
L92	RKC193	L102	RKC203	L112	RKC213	L122	RKC223	L132	RKC233
L93	RKC194	L103	RKC204	L113	RKC214	L123	RKC224	L133	RKC234
L94	RKC195	L104	RKC205	L114	RKC215	L124	RKC225	L134	RKC235
L95	RKC196	L105	RKC206	L115	RKC216	L125	RKC226	L135	RKC236
L96	RKC197	L106	RKC207	L116	RKC217	L126	RKC227	L136	RKC237
L97	RKC198	L107	RKC208	L117	RKC218	L127	RKC228	L137	RKC238
L98	RKC199	L108	RKC209	L118	RKC219	L128	RKC229	L138	RKC239
L99	RKC200	L109	RKC210	L119	RKC220	L129	RKC230	L139	RKC240
L100	RKC201	L110	RKC211	L120	RKC221	L130	RKC231	L140	RKC241

L142-L170 Leyland Titan PD2/20 Alexander H32/26R 1954-55

L142	RKC243	L148	RKC249	L154	RKC255	L160	RKC261	L166	RKC267
L143	RKC244	L149	RKC250	L155	RKC256	L161	RKC262	L167	RKC268
L144	RKC245	L150	RKC251	L156	RKC257	L162	RKC263	L168	RKC269
L145	RKC246	L151	RKC252	L157	RKC258	L163	RKC264	L169	RKC270
L146	RKC247	L152	RKC253	L158	RKC259	L164	RKC265	L170	RKC271
L147	RKC248	L153	RKC254	L159	RKC260	L165	RKC266		

XL171	SKB168	Leyland Royal Tiger PSU1/13	Crossley	C44F	1956
XL172	SKB169	Leyland Royal Tiger PSU1/13	Crossley	C44F	1956
XL173	SKB170	Leyland Royal Tiger PSU1/13	Crossley	C44F	1956
XL174	SKB171	Leyland Royal Tiger PSU1/13	Crossley	C44F	1956
SL175	SKB172	Leyland Royal Tiger PSU1/13	Crossley	DP40F	1956
SL176	SKB173	Leyland Royal Tiger PSU1/13	Crossley	DP40F	1956

L177-L211   Leyland Titan PD2/20   Weymann Orion   H32/26R   1955

L177	SKB174	L184	SKB181	L191	SKB188	L198	SKB195	L205	SKB202
L178	SKB175	L185	SKB182	L192	SKB189	L199	SKB196	L206	SKB203
L179	SKB176	L186	SKB183	L193	SKB190	L200	SKB197	L207	SKB204
L180	SKB177	L187	SKB184	L194	SKB191	L201	SKB198	L208	SKB205
L181	SKB178	L188	SKB185	L195	SKB192	L202	SKB199	L209	SKB206
L182	SKB179	L189	SKB186	L196	SKB193	L203	SKB200	L210	SKB207
L183	SKB180	L190	SKB187	L197	SKB194	L204	SKB201	L211	SKB208

L212-L229   Leyland Titan PD2/20   Crossley   H32/26R   1955-56

L212	SKB209	L216	SKB213	L220	SKB217	L224	SKB221	L227	SKB224
L213	SKB210	L217	SKB214	L221	SKB218	L225	SKB222	L228	SKB225
L214	SKB211	L218	SKB215	L222	SKB219	L226	SKB223	L229	SKB226
L215	SKB212	L219	SKB216	L223	SKB220				

L230-L244   Leyland Titan PD2/20   Crossley/LCPT   H32/26R   1956

L230	SKB227	L233	SKB230	L236	SKB233	L239	SKB236	L242	SKB239
L231	SKB228	L234	SKB231	L237	SKB234	L240	SKB237	L243	SKB240
L232	SKB229	L235	SKB232	L238	SKB235	L241	SKB238	L244	SKB241

L245-L279   Leyland Titan PD2/20   Crossley   H33/29R   1956-57

L245	VKB701	L252	VKB708	L259	VKB715	L266	VKB722	L273	VKB729
L246	VKB702	L253	VKB709	L260	VKB716	L267	VKB723	L274	VKB730
L247	VKB703	L254	VKB710	L261	VKB717	L268	VKB724	L275	VKB731
L248	VKB704	L255	VKB711	L262	VKB718	L269	VKB725	L276	VKB732
L249	VKB705	L256	VKB712	L263	VKB719	L270	VKB726	L277	VKB733
L250	VKB706	L257	VKB713	L264	VKB720	L271	VKB727	L278	VKB734
L251	VKB707	L258	VKB714	L265	VKB721	L272	VKB728	L279	VKB735

L280-L285   Leyland Titan PD2/20   Crossley/MCCW   H35/29R   1961

L280	VKB736	L282	VKB738	L283	VKB739	L284	VKB740	L285	VKB741
L281	VKB737								

L286-L309   Leyland Titan PD2/30   Crossley/MCCW   H35/29R   1961

L286	VKB742	L291	VKB747	L296	VKB752	L301	VKB757	L306	VKB762
L287	VKB743	L292	VKB748	L297	VKB753	L302	VKB758	L307	VKB763
L288	VKB744	L293	VKB749	L298	VKB754	L303	VKB759	L308	VKB764
L289	VKB745	L294	VKB750	L299	VKB755	L304	VKB760	L309	VKB765
L290	VKB746	L295	VKB751	L300	VKB756	L305	VKB761		

L310-L344   Leyland Titan PD2/20   Crossley   H33/29R   1957-58

L310	VKB831	L317	VKB838	L324	VKB845	L331	VKB852	L338	VKB859
L311	VKB832	L318	VKB839	L325	VKB846	L332	VKB853	L339	VKB860
L312	VKB833	L319	VKB840	L326	VKB847	L333	VKB854	L340	VKB861
L313	VKB834	L320	VKB841	L327	VKB848	L334	VKB855	L341	VKB862
L314	VKB835	L321	VKB842	L328	VKB849	L335	VKB856	L342	VKB863
L315	VKB836	L322	VKB843	L329	VKB850	L336	VKB857	L343	VKB864
L316	VKB837	L323	VKB844	L330	VKB851	L337	VKB858	L344	VKB865

L345-L369   Leyland Titan PD2/30   Crossley   H33/29R   1958

L345	WKF201	L350	WKF206	L355	WKF211	L360	WKF216	L365	WKF221
L346	WKF202	L351	WKF207	L356	WKF212	L361	WKF217	L366	WKF222
L347	WKF203	L352	WKF208	L357	WKF213	L362	WKF218	L367	WKF223
L348	WKF204	L353	WKF209	L358	WKF214	L363	WKF219	L368	WKF224
L349	WKF205	L354	WKF210	L359	WKF215	L364	WKF220	L369	WKF225

L370-L410   Leyland Titan PD2/12   Weymann Aurora   H30/26R   1952

L370	MKB890	L376	MKB896	L383	MKB903	L390	MKB910	L395	MKB915
L371	MKB891	L377	MKB897	L384	MKB904	L391	MKB911	L396	MKB916
L372	MKB892	L378	MKB898	L387	MKB907	L392	MKB912	L401	MKB921
L373	MKB893	L379	MKB899	L388	MKB908	L393	MKB913	L406	MKB926
L374	MKB894	L380	MKB900	L389	MKB909	L394	MKB914	L410	MKB930
L375	MKB895	L381	MKB901						

L500-L699   Leyland Atlantean PDR1/1   Metro-Cammell   H43/33F   1962-64

L500	500KD	L540	540KD	L580	580KD	L620	620KD	L660	660KD
L501	501KD	L541	541KD	L581	581KD	L621	621KD	L661	661KD
L502	502KD	L542	542KD	L582	582KD	L622	622KD	L662	662KD
L503	503KD	L543	543KD	L583	583KD	L623	623KD	L663	663KD
L504	504KD	L544	544KD	L584	584KD	L624	624KD	L664	664KD
L505	505KD	L545	545KD	L585	585KD	L625	625KD	L665	665KD
L506	506KD	L546	546KD	L586	586KD	L626	626KD	L666	666KD
L507	507KD	L547	547KD	L587	587KD	L627	627KD	L667	667KD
L508	508KD	L548	548KD	L588	588KD	L628	628KD	L668	668KD
L509	509KD	L549	549KD	L589	589KD	L629	629KD	L669	669KD
L510	510KD	L550	550KD	L590	590KD	L630	630KD	L670	670KD
L511	511KD	L551	551KD	L591	591KD	L631	631KD	L671	671KD
L512	512KD	L552	552KD	L592	592KD	L632	632KD	L672	672KD
L513	513KD	L553	553KD	L593	593KD	L633	633KD	L673	673KD
L514	514KD	L554	554KD	L594	594KD	L634	634KD	L674	674KD
L515	515KD	L555	555KD	L595	595KD	L635	635KD	L675	675KD
L516	516KD	L556	556KD	L596	596KD	L636	636KD	L676	676KD
L517	517KD	L557	557KD	L597	597KD	L637	637KD	L677	677KD
L518	518KD	L558	558KD	L598	598KD	L638	638KD	L678	678KD
L519	519KD	L559	559KD	L599	599KD	L639	639KD	L679	679KD
L520	520KD	L560	560KD	L600	600KD	L640	640KD	L680	680KD
L521	521KD	L561	561KD	L601	601KD	L641	641KD	L681	681KD
L522	522KD	L562	562KD	L602	602KD	L642	642KD	L682	682KD
L523	523KD	L563	563KD	L603	603KD	L643	643KD	L683	683KD
L524	524KD	L564	564KD	L604	604KD	L644	644KD	L684	684KD
L525	525KD	L565	565KD	L605	605KD	L645	645KD	L685	685KD
L526	526KD	L566	566KD	L606	606KD	L646	646KD	L686	686KD
L527	527KD	L567	567KD	L607	607KD	L647	647KD	L687	687KD
L528	528KD	L568	568KD	L608	608KD	L648	648KD	L688	688KD
L529	529KD	L569	569KD	L609	609KD	L649	649KD	L689	689KD
L530	530KD	L570	570KD	L610	610KD	L650	650KD	L690	690KD
L531	531KD	L571	571KD	L611	611KD	L651	651KD	L691	691KD
L532	532KD	L572	572KD	L612	612KD	L652	652KD	L692	692KD
L533	533KD	L573	573KD	L613	613KD	L653	653KD	L693	693KD
L534	534KD	L574	574KD	L614	614KD	L654	654KD	L694	694KD
L535	535KD	L575	575KD	L615	615KD	L655	655KD	L695	695KD
L536	536KD	L576	576KD	L616	616KD	L656	656KD	L696	696KD
L537	537KD	L577	577KD	L617	617KD	L657	657KD	L697	697KD
L538	538KD	L578	578KD	L618	618KD	L658	658KD	L698	698KD
L539	539KD	L579	579KD	L619	619KD	L659	659KD	L699	699KD

Opposite, top: **Some in the bus industry believed that the bulge below the cab which was a feature of most new-look fronts detracted from the profile of the bus. Liverpool had its own ideas on frontal styling as L358, a 1958 Titan PD2 with Crossley bodywork, illustrates. Whether the unbroken front profile is an improvement is open to question.** *Reg Wilson*

Opposite, bottom: **Liverpool took a fresh look at body design when it placed its first big order for 200 Atlanteans. Metro-Cammell got the body order, and produced a design that was both attractive and practical with its flat windscreens.** *Iain MacGregor*

L700-L879   Leyland Atlantean PDR1/1   Metro-Cammell   H43/35F*   1966-67   *L724/63/79/83/8 are H43/33F

L700	CKF700C	L736	CKF736C	L772	FKF772D	L808	FKF808D	L844	FKF844E
L701	CKF701C	L737	CKF737C	L773	FKF773D	L809	FKF809D	L845	FKF845E
L702	CKF702C	L738	CKF738C	L774	FKF774D	L810	FKF810D	L846	FKF846E
L703	CKF703C	L739	CKF739C	L775	FKF775D	L811	FKF811D	L847	FKF847E
L704	CKF704C	L740	CKF740C	L776	FKF776D	L812	FKF812D	L848	FKF848E
L705	CKF705D	L741	CKF741C	L777	FKF777D	L813	FKF813D	L849	FKF849E
L706	CKF706C	L742	CKF742C	L778	FKF778D	L814	FKF814D	L850	FKF850E
L707	CKF707C	L743	CKF743C	L779	FKF779D	L815	FKF815D	L851	FKF851E
L708	CKF708C	L744	CKF744C	L780	FKF780D	L816	FKF816D	L852	FKF852E
L709	CKF709C	L745	CKF745C	L781	FKF781D	L817	FKF817D	L853	FKF853E
L710	CKF710C	L746	CKF746C	L782	FKF782D	L818	FKF818D	L854	FKF854E
L711	CKF711C	L747	CKF747C	L783	FKF783D	L819	FKF819D	L855	FKF855E
L712	CKF712C	L748	CKF748C	L784	FKF784D	L820	FKF820D	L856	FKF856E
L713	CKF713C	L749	CKF749C	L785	FKF785D	L821	FKF821D	L857	FKF857E
L714	CKF714C	L750	CKF750C	L786	FKF786D	L822	FKF822D	L858	FKF858E
L715	CKF715C	L751	CKF751C	L787	FKF787D	L823	FKF823D	L859	FKF859E
L716	CKF716C	L752	CKF752C	L788	FKF788D	L824	FKF824D	L860	FKF860E
L717	CKF717C	L753	CKF753C	L789	FKF789D	L825	FKF825E	L861	FKF861E
L718	CKF718C	L754	CKF754D	L790	FKF790D	L826	FKF826D	L862	FKF862E
L719	CKF719D	L755	CKF755D	L791	FKF791D	L827	FKF827D	L863	FKF863E
L720	CKF720D	L756	CKF756D	L792	FKF792D	L828	FKF828E	L864	FKF864E
L721	CKF721C	L757	CKF757D	L793	FKF793D	L829	FKF829D	L865	FKF865E
L722	CKF722D	L758	CKF758D	L794	FKF794D	L830	FKF830E	L866	FKF866E
L723	CKF723C	L759	CKF759D	L795	FKF795D	L831	FKF831E	L867	FKF867E
L724	CKF724D	L760	FKF760D	L796	FKF796D	L832	FKF832E	L868	FKF868E
L725	CKF725C	L761	FKF761D	L797	FKF797D	L833	FKF833E	L869	FKF869E
L726	CKF726C	L762	FKF762D	L798	FKF798D	L834	FKF834E	L870	FKF870E
L727	CKF727D	L763	FKF763D	L799	FKF799D	L835	FKF835E	L871	FKF871E
L728	CKF728C	L764	FKF764D	L800	FKF800D	L836	FKF836E	L872	FKF872E
L720	CKF729D	L765	FKF765D	L801	FKF801D	L837	FKF837E	L873	FKF873E
L730	CKF730C	L766	FKF766D	L802	FKF802D	L838	FKF838E	L874	FKF874E
L731	CKF731C	L767	FKF767D	L803	FKF803D	L839	FKF839E	L875	FKF875E
L732	CKF732C	L768	FKF768D	L804	FKF804D	L840	FKF840E	L876	FKF876E
L733	CKF733C	L769	FKF769D	L805	FKF805D	L841	FKF841E	L877	FKF877E
L734	CKF734D	L770	FKF770D	L806	FKF806D	L842	FKF842E	L878	FKF878E
L735	CKF735C	L771	FKF771D	L807	FKF807D	L843	FKF843E	L879	FKF879E

An early English order for Scottish-based coachbuilder Walter Alexander saw 60 bodies being delivered to Liverpool Corporation in 1954-55. They were on Leyland Titan PD2/20 chassis.
Roy Marshall

The characteristic Liverpool bus in 1968 was the Leyland Atlantean with peak-domed Metro-Cammell body. There were 380 in service, all broadly similar although with detail differences between batches. A switch to single-deckers in 1968 brought to an end production of this distinctive style of body. *Roy Marshall*

1001-1070 Leyland Panther PSUR1A/1 Metro-Cammell B47D 1968

1001	FKF880F	1015	FKF894F	1029	FKF908F	1043	FKF922F	1057	FKF936G
1002	FKF881F	1016	FKF895F	1030	FKF909F	1044	FKF923F	1058	FKF937G
1003	FKF882F	1017	FKF896F	1031	FKF910F	1045	FKF924F	1059	FKF938G
1004	FKF883F	1018	FKF897F	1032	FKF911F	1046	FKF925F	1060	FKF939G
1005	FKF884F	1019	FKF898F	1033	FKF912F	1047	FKF926F	1061	FKF940G
1006	FKF885F	1020	FKF899F	1034	FKF913F	1048	FKF927F	1062	FKF941G
1007	FKF886F	1021	FKF900F	1035	FKF914G	1049	FKF928F	1063	FKF942G
1008	FKF887F	1022	FKF901F	1036	FKF915F	1050	FKF929F	1064	FKF943G
1009	FKF888F	1023	FKF902F	1037	FKF916F	1051	FKF930F	1065	FKF944G
1010	FKF889F	1024	FKF903F	1038	FKF917F	1052	FKF931G	1066	FKF945G
1011	FKF890F	1025	FKF904F	1039	FKF918F	1053	FKF932G	1067	FKF946G
1012	FKF891F	1026	FKF905F	1040	FKF919F	1054	FKF933G	1068	FKF947G
1013	FKF892F	1027	FKF906F	1041	FKF920F	1055	FKF934G	1069	FKF948G
1014	FKF893F	1028	FKF907F	1042	FKF921F	1056	FKF935G	1070	FKF949G

1071-1110 Leyland Panther PSUR1A/1 Metro-Cammell B47D 1968-69

1071	RKA950G	1079	RKA958G	1087	RKA966G	1095	RKA974G	1103	RKA982G
1072	RKA951G	1080	RKA959G	1088	RKA967G	1096	RKA975G	1104	RKA983G
1073	RKA952G	1081	RKA960G	1089	RKA968G	1097	RKA976G	1105	RKA984G
1074	RKA953G	1082	RKA961G	1090	RKA969G	1098	RKA977G	1106	RKA985G
1075	RKA954G	1083	RKA962G	1091	RKA970G	1099	RKA978G	1107	RKA986G
1076	RKA955G	1084	RKA963G	1092	RKA971G	1100	RKA979G	1108	RKA987G
1077	RKA956G	1085	RKA964G	1093	RKA972G	1101	RKA980G	1109	RKA988G
1078	RKA957G	1086	RKA965G	1094	RKA973G	1102	RKA981G	1110	RKA989G

On order: 25 Bristol RE with Park Royal bodywork

Livery: Green and cream

LYTHAM ST ANNES

Lytham St Annes Corporation Transport Department, 300 Lytham Road, Blackpool

In April 1922 the two neighbouring urban district councils of Lytham and St Annes were merged. St Annes was a tramway operator - just - having taken over the operations of the Blackpool, St Annes and Lytham Tramways Co in November 1921, along with 40 electric trams. The tramway system closed in 1937.

Lytham St Annes' first buses were six Guys in 1923; by 1931 there were 15 Guys in the fleet. Additional second-hand Guys were purchased in the early 1930s, but from 1933 all new additions to the fleet were Leylands, apart from two wartime Daimlers. The first double-deckers were five Titans in 1936, which had Leyland bodies with full-width cabs, no doubt inspired by neighbouring Blackpool. These, and nine similar buses in 1937, were long-lived, typically giving 25 years service.

Titans dominated Lytham St Annes' postwar purchases, with the last being delivered in 1964.

The future: In 1974 the newly-created Fylde Borough Council took over, and in 1986 the operation became Fylde Borough Transport Ltd. The council-owned company was privatised in a management buy-out in December 1993, but its independence was short-lived. In May 1994 it was taken over by Blackpool Transport Services - ironically bringing it back into the public sector.

In 1968 the fleet operated by Lytham St Annes retained many of the all-Leyland double-deck Titans, though withdrawal of the type had commenced. Pictured in St Annes Square just before withdrawal is PD2/1 number 10, which was new in 1948.
Roy Marshall

In 1960 Lytham St Annes added six Titans to its fleet. These were conservative PD2/30s with synchromesh gearboxes and vacuum brakes. They had Metro-Cammell Orion bodies. *Reg Wilson*

5-9			Leyland Titan PD2/12		Leyland		H33/26R	1951	
5	NTD574	6	NTD575	7	NTD576	8	NTD577	9	NTD578

10	JTD381	Leyland Titan PD2/1	Leyland	H30/26R	1948
11	JTD382	Leyland Titan PD2/1	Leyland	H30/26R	1948
13	JTD384	Leyland Titan PD2/1	Leyland	H30/26R	1948
14	JTD385	Leyland Titan PD2/1	Leyland	H30/26R	1948

16-21			Leyland Titan PD1		Leyland		H30/26R	1946	
16	GTB906	18	GTB905	19	GTB903	20	GTB907	21	GTB908
17	GTB904								

23	EED4	Leyland Titan PD1	Alexander/Leyland	H30/26R	1946	Warrington Corporation, 1962	
24	EED5	Leyland Titan PD1	Alexander/Leyland	H30/26R	1946	Warrington Corporation, 1962	
54	367BTJ	Leyland Tiger Cub PSUC1/1	Burlingham	B42F	1957		
55	368BTJ	Leyland Tiger Cub PSUC1/1	Burlingham	B42F	1957		
56	369BTJ	Leyland Tiger Cub PSUC1/1	Burlingham	B42F	1957		

57-61			Leyland Titan PD2/20		Northern Counties		H33/28R	1957	
57	756CTD	58	757CTD	59	758CTD	60	759CTD	61	760CTD

62-67			Leyland Titan PD2/30		Metro-Cammell		H35/28R	1960	
62	45NTD	64	47NTD	65	48NTD	66	49NTD	67	50NTD
63	46NTD								

68	CTF625B	Leyland Titan PD2A/27	Massey	H37/27F	1964
69	CTF626B	Leyland Titan PD2A/27	Massey	H37/27F	1964
70	CTF627B	Leyland Titan PD2A/27	Massey	H37/27F	1964

Livery: Blue and white

MANCHESTER

City of Manchester Transport, Devonshire Street, Manchester

Manchester Corporation took over the operations of the Manchester Carriage and Tramways Co, introducing electric trams to the city's streets in 1901. Three double-deck motorbuses were purchased in 1906 although operation came to a halt when war broke out in 1914. Motorbus operation restarted in 1917 and expanded rapidly, with much joint-working of express services between the city and its satellite towns.

A new general manager in 1929, R Stuart Pilcher, favoured buses over trams, and the first tram to bus conversion took place in 1930. Some small operators' services were acquired during the early 1930s.

A new streamlined double-deck body was designed by Manchester and appeared in 1936, setting new standards of appearance for the city's fleet. Trolleybus operation was started in 1938. Motorbuses in this period were being supplied by Crossley and Leyland, and these two manufacturers also provided the undertaking's first trolleybuses.

The last Manchester tram ran in 1949 while the last trolleybuses, 62 BUTs, entered service in 1955-56. Trolleybus operation ceased at the end of 1966.

The main postwar suppliers of Manchester's buses were Leyland and Daimler, although Crossley figured strongly until 1949. Body orders went to a number of builders, but Metro-Cammell was the main supplier from 1950. However when a new generation of distinctively-styled two-door double-deckers was ordered for 1968 delivery the bodywork was supplied by Park Royal, a company which had previously only built single-deck bodywork for Manchester. The new Mancunians of 1968 were as advanced as the previous streamlined model had been three decades before.

Manchester Corporation was one of very few municipal fleets to buy three-axle Bedford VAL coaches.

The future: Manchester Corporation Transport was the biggest constituent of the new SELNEC PTE, set up in November 1969.

8-23		Leyland Royal Tiger PSU1/13	Northen Counties	B42R*	1953	*20-23 are B43F
8	NNB108	15	NNB115	17	NNB117	20	NNB120	22	NNB122
12	NNB112	16	NNB116	18	NNB118	21	NNB121	23	NNB123

33	NNB133	Leyland Royal Tiger PSU1/13	Burlingham	C41F	1953
34	NNB134	Leyland Royal Tiger PSU1/13	Burlingham	C41F	1953
36	NNB136	Leyland Tiger Cub PSUC1/1	Burlingham	C41F	1956
37	NNB137	Leyland Tiger Cub PSUC1/1	Burlingham	C41F	1956
38	NNB138	Leyland Tiger Cub PSUC1/1	Burlingham	C41F	1956
39	NNB139	Leyland Tiger Cub PSUC1/1	Burlingham	C41F	1956

Opposite: **The first break from the original flat-fronted body style on rear-engined buses for Manchester came in 1964 with the delivery of Metro-Cammell bodies of this style on Atlantean and Fleetline chassis. This is a Fleetline. Manchester was one of the early proponents of one-man-operation of busy urban services, and in 1967 added 29 Leyland Panthers to its fleet. These had two-door 44-seat Metro-Cammell bodies and a bright new livery.** *Omnicolour/Martin Llewellyn/Bill Potter*

The 1968 North West Bus Handbook

Intended for airport services, Manchester's 1962 Tiger Cubs originally operated in this blue livery. They had Park Royal bodies with 36 generously-spaced high-backed seats at a time when the standard layout for this type of body was 45 bus seats. *Reg Wilson*

40-45

Albion Aberdonian MR11L   Seddon   B42F   1958

40	UXJ240	**42**	UXJ242	**43**	UXJ243	**44**	UXJ244	**45**	UXJ245
41	UXJ241								

46-50

Leyland Tiger Cub PSUC1/2   Park Royal   DP40F   1961

46	9746NA	**47**	9747NA	**48**	9748NA	**49**	9749NA	**50**	9750NA

51-60

Leyland Tiger Cub PSUC1/12   Park Royal   B38D*   1962   *51-4 are DP36F

51	3651NE	**53**	3653NE	**55**	3655NE	**57**	3657NE	**59**	3659NE
52	3652NE	**54**	3654NE	**56**	3656NE	**58**	3658NE	**60**	3660NE

61-80

Leyland Panther Cub PSRC1/1   Park Royal   B43D   1964-65

61	ANF161B	**65**	BND865C	**69**	BND869C	**73**	BND873C	**77**	BND877C
62	ANF162B	**66**	BND866C	**70**	BND870C	**74**	BND874C	**78**	BND878C
63	BND863C	**67**	BND867C	**71**	BND871C	**75**	BND875C	**79**	BND879C
64	BND864C	**68**	BND868C	**72**	BND872C	**76**	BND876C	**80**	BND880C

81-110

Leyland Panther PSUR1/1   Metro-Cammell   B44D   1967

81	GND81E	**87**	GND87E	**93**	GND93E	**99**	GND99E	**106**	GND106E
82	GND82E	**88**	GND88E	**94**	GND94E	**101**	GND101E	**107**	GND107E
83	GND83E	**89**	GND89E	**95**	GND95E	**102**	GND102E	**108**	GND108E
84	GND84E	**90**	GND90E	**96**	GND96E	**103**	GND103E	**109**	GND109E
85	GND85E	**91**	GND91E	**97**	GND97E	**104**	GND104E	**110**	GND110E
86	GND86E	**92**	GND92E	**98**	GND98E	**105**	GND105E		

201-206

Bedford VAL14 — Plaxton Panorama — C47F* — 1966 — *203 is C45F

201	GNB516D	203	GNB517D	204	GND112E	205	GNB518D	206	GND113E
202	GND111E								

207-212

Bedford VAL70 — Plaxton Panorama Elite — C52F — 1967

207	JND207F	209	JND209F	210	JND210F	211	JND211F	212	JND212F
208	JND208F								

1001-1048

Leyland Atlantean PDR1/1 — Park Royal — H45/28D — 1968

1001	HVM901F	1011	HVM911F	1021	HVM921F	1031	HVM931F	1040	HVM940F
1002	HVM902F	1012	HVM912F	1022	HVM922F	1032	HVM932F	1041	HVM941F
1003	HVM903F	1013	HVM913F	1023	HVM923F	1033	HVM933F	1042	HVM942F
1004	HVM904F	1014	HVM914F	1024	HVM924F	1034	HVM934F	1043	HVM943F
1005	HVM905F	1015	HVM915F	1025	HVM925F	1035	HVM935F	1044	HVM944F
1006	HVM906F	1016	HVM916F	1026	HVM926F	1036	HVM936F	1045	HVM945F
1007	HVM907F	1017	HVM917F	1027	HVM927F	1037	HVM937F	1046	HVM946F
1008	HVM908F	1018	HVM918F	1028	HVM928F	1038	HVM938F	1047	HVM947F
1009	HVM909F	1019	HVM919F	1029	HVM929F	1039	HVM939F	1048	HVM948F
1010	HVM910F	1020	HVM920F	1030	HVM930F				

2001-2048

Daimler Fleetline CRG6LX — Park Royal — H45/28D — 1968

2001	HVM801F	2011	HVM811F	2021	HVM821F	2031	HVM831F	2040	HVM840F
2002	HVM802F	2012	HVM812F	2022	HVM822F	2032	HVM832F	2041	HVM841F
2003	HVM803F	2013	HVM813F	2023	HVM823F	2033	HVM833F	2042	HVM842F
2004	HVM804F	2014	HVM814F	2024	HVM824F	2034	HVM834F	2043	HVM843F
2005	HVM805F	2015	HVM815F	2025	HVM825F	2035	HVM835F	2044	HVM844F
2006	HVM806F	2016	HVM816F	2026	HVM826F	2036	HVM836F	2045	HVM845F
2007	HVM807F	2017	HVM817F	2027	HVM827F	2037	HVM837F	2046	HVM846F
2008	HVM808F	2018	HVM818F	2028	HVM828F	2038	HVM838F	2047	HVM847F
2009	HVM809F	2019	HVM819F	2029	HVM829F	2039	HVM839F	2048	HVM848F
2010	HVM810F	2020	HVM820F	2030	HVM830F				

3050-3098

Leyland Titan PD1/3 — Metro-Cammell — H32/26R — 1947-48

3050	GVR252	3053	GVR255	3064	GVR266	3086	GVR288	3095	GVR297
3051	GVR253	3054	GVR256	3065	GVR267	3092	GVR294	3098	GVR300
3052	GVR254	3063	GVR265	3081	GVR283				

3122-3199

Leyland Titan PD1/3 — Metro-Cammell — H32/26R — 1949

3122	JNA423	3139	JNA440	3155	JNA456	3170	JNA471	3185	JNA486
3124	JNA425	3140	JNA441	3156	JNA457	3171	JNA472	3186	JNA487
3125	JNA426	3141	JNA442	3157	JNA458	3172	JNA473	3187	JNA488
3126	JNA427	3142	JNA443	3158	JNA459	3173	JNA474	3188	JNA489
3127	JNA428	3143	JNA444	3159	JNA460	3174	JNA475	3189	JNA490
3128	JNA429	3144	JNA445	3160	JNA461	3175	JNA476	3190	JNA491
3129	JNA430	3145	JNA446	3161	JNA462	3176	JNA477	3191	JNA492
3130	JNA431	3146	JNA447	3162	JNA463	3177	JNA478	3192	JNA493
3131	JNA432	3147	JNA448	3163	JNA464	3178	JNA479	3193	JNA494
3132	JNA433	3148	JNA449	3164	JNA465	3179	JNA480	3194	JNA495
3133	JNA434	3149	JNA450	3165	JNA466	3180	JNA481	3195	JNA496
3134	JNA435	3150	JNA451	3166	JNA467	3181	JNA482	3196	JNA497
3135	JNA436	3151	JNA452	3167	JNA468	3182	JNA483	3197	JNA498
3136	JNA437	3152	JNA453	3168	JNA469	3183	JNA484	3198	JNA499
3137	JNA438	3153	JNA454	3169	JNA470	3184	JNA485	3199	JNA500
3138	JNA439	3154	JNA455						

Parrs Wood depot abuts the main London-Manchester rail line and its allocation comprised mostly Leyland products, including 3416, a Titan PD2/12 with Metro-Cammell bodywork. *Bill Potter*

3200-3264   Leyland Titan PD2/3   Metro-Cammell   H32/26R   1951

3200	JND601	3213	JND614	3226	JND627	3239	JND640	3252	JND653
3201	JND602	3214	JND615	3227	JND628	3240	JND641	3253	JND654
3202	JND603	3215	JND616	3228	JND629	3241	JND642	3254	JND655
3203	JND604	3216	JND617	3229	JND630	3242	JND643	3255	JND656
3204	JND605	3217	JND618	3230	JND631	3243	JND644	3256	JND657
3205	JND606	3218	JND619	3231	JND632	3244	JND645	3257	JND658
3206	JND607	3219	JND620	3232	JND633	3245	JND646	3258	JND659
3207	JND608	3220	JND621	3233	JND634	3246	JND647	3259	JND660
3208	JND609	3221	JND622	3234	JND635	3247	JND648	3260	JND661
3209	JND610	3222	JND623	3235	JND636	3248	JND649	3261	JND662
3210	JND611	3223	JND624	3236	JND637	3249	JND650	3262	JND663
3211	JND612	3224	JND625	3237	JND638	3250	JND651	3263	JND664
3212	JND613	3225	JND626	3238	JND639	3251	JND652	3264	JND665

3265-3299   Leyland Titan PD2/3   Leyland Farington   H32/26R   1950

3265	JND666	3272	JND673	3279	JND680	3286	JND687	3293	JND694
3266	JND667	3273	JND674	3280	JND681	3287	JND688	3294	JND695
3267	JND668	3274	JND675	3281	JND682	3288	JND689	3295	JND696
3268	JND669	3275	JND676	3282	JND683	3289	JND690	3296	JND697
3269	JND670	3276	JND677	3283	JND684	3290	JND691	3297	JND698
3270	JND671	3277	JND678	3284	JND685	3291	JND692	3298	JND699
3271	JND672	3278	JND679	3285	JND686	3292	JND693	3299	JND700

3300-3329   Leyland Titan PD2/12   Northern Counties   H32/28R*   1953-54   *3323-5/7-9 are H33/28R

3300	NNB140	3306	NNB146	3312	NNB152	3318	NNB158	3324	NNB164
3301	NNB141	3307	NNB147	3313	NNB153	3319	NNB159	3325	NNB165
3302	NNB142	3308	NNB148	3314	NNB154	3320	NNB160	3326	NNB166
3303	NNB143	3309	NNB149	3315	NNB155	3321	NNB161	3327	NNB167
3304	NNB144	3310	NNB150	3316	NNB156	3322	NNB162	3328	NNB168
3305	NNB145	3311	NNB151	3317	NNB157	3323	NNB163	3329	NNB169

The main link between Altrincham and Manchester is the high frequency service 64, the preserve of Daimler buses from Princess Road depot. Seen at the Manchester end of the service is 4466. *Bill Potter*

3330-3369   Leyland Titan PD2/12   Leyland   H32/28R   1953

3330	NNB170	3338	NNB178	3346	NNB186	3354	NNB194	3362	NNB202
3331	NNB171	3339	NNB179	3347	NNB187	3355	NNB195	3364	NNB204
3332	NNB172	3340	NNB180	3348	NNB188	3356	NNB196	3365	NNB205
3333	NNB173	3341	NNB181	3349	NNB189	3357	NNB197	3366	NNB206
3334	NNB174	3342	NNB182	3350	NNB190	3358	NNB198	3367	NNB207
3335	NNB175	3343	NNB183	3351	NNB191	3359	NNB199	3368	NNB208
3336	NNB176	3344	NNB184	3352	NNB192	3360	NNB200	3369	NNB209
3337	NNB177	3345	NNB185	3353	NNB193	3361	NNB201		

3411-3470   Leyland Titan PD2/12   Metro-Cammell   H36/28R   1956

3411	PND411	3423	PND423	3435	PND435	3447	PND447	3459	PND459
3412	PND412	3424	PND424	3436	PND436	3448	PND448	3460	PND460
3413	PND413	3425	PND425	3437	PND437	3449	PND449	3461	PND461
3414	PND414	3426	PND426	3438	PND438	3450	PND450	3462	PND462
3415	PND415	3427	PND427	3439	PND439	3451	PND451	3463	PND463
3416	PND416	3428	PND428	3440	PND440	3452	PND452	3464	PND464
3417	PND417	3429	PND429	3441	PND441	3453	PND453	3465	PND465
3418	PND418	3430	PND430	3442	PND442	3454	PND454	3466	PND466
3419	PND419	3431	PND431	3443	PND443	3455	PND455	3467	PND467
3420	PND420	3432	PND432	3444	PND444	3456	PND456	3468	PND468
3421	PND421	3433	PND433	3445	PND445	3457	PND457	3469	PND469
3422	PND422	3434	PND434	3446	PND446	3458	PND458	3470	PND470

3471-3514 — Leyland Titan PD2/40 — Burlingham — H37/28R — 1958

3471	TNA471	3480	TNA480	3489	TNA489	3498	TNA498	3507	TNA507
3472	TNA472	3481	TNA481	3490	TNA490	3499	TNA499	3508	TNA508
3473	TNA473	3482	TNA482	3491	TNA491	3500	TNA500	3509	TNA509
3474	TNA474	3483	TNA483	3492	TNA492	3501	TNA501	3510	TNA510
3475	TNA475	3484	TNA484	3493	TNA493	3502	TNA502	3511	TNA511
3476	TNA476	3485	TNA485	3494	TNA494	3503	TNA503	3512	TNA512
3477	TNA477	3486	TNA486	3495	TNA495	3504	TNA504	3513	TNA513
3478	TNA478	3487	TNA487	3496	TNA496	3505	TNA505	3514	TNA514
3479	TNA479	3488	TNA488	3497	TNA497	3506	TNA506		

3515-3520 — Leyland Titan PD2/34 — Burlingham — H37/28R — 1958

3515	TNA515	3517	TNA517	3518	TNA518	3519	TNA519	3520	TNA520
3516	TNA516								

3521-3620 — Leyland Titan PD2/40 — Metro-Cammell — H37/28R — 1958-59

3521	UNB521	3541	UNB541	3561	UNB561	3581	UNB581	3601	UNB601
3522	UNB522	3542	UNB542	3562	UNB562	3582	UNB582	3602	UNB602
3523	UNB523	3543	UNB543	3563	UNB563	3583	UNB583	3603	UNB603
3524	UNB524	3544	UNB544	3564	UNB564	3584	UNB584	3604	UNB604
3525	UNB525	3545	UNB545	3565	UNB565	3585	UNB585	3605	UNB605
3526	UNB526	3546	UNB546	3566	UNB566	3586	UNB586	3606	UNB606
3527	UNB527	3547	UNB547	3567	UNB567	3587	UNB587	3607	UNB607
3528	UNB528	3548	UNB548	3568	UNB568	3588	UNB588	3608	UNB608
3529	UNB529	3549	UNB549	3569	UNB569	3589	UNB589	3609	UNB609
3530	UNB530	3550	UNB550	3570	UNB570	3590	UNB590	3610	UNB610
3531	UNB531	3551	UNB551	3571	UNB571	3591	UNB591	3611	UNB611
3532	UNB532	3552	UNB552	3572	UNB572	3592	UNB592	3612	UNB612
3533	UNB533	3553	UNB553	3573	UNB573	3593	UNB593	3613	UNB613
3534	UNB534	3554	UNB554	3574	UNB574	3594	UNB594	3614	UNB614
3535	UNB535	3555	UNB555	3575	UNB575	3595	UNB595	3615	UNB615
3536	UNB536	3556	UNB556	3576	UNB576	3596	UNB596	3616	UNB616
3537	UNB537	3557	UNB557	3577	UNB577	3597	UNB597	3617	UNB617
3538	UNB538	3558	UNB558	3578	UNB578	3598	UNB598	3618	UNB618
3539	UNB539	3559	UNB559	3579	UNB579	3599	UNB599	3619	UNB619
3540	UNB540	3560	UNB560	3580	UNB580	3600	UNB600	3620	UNB620

3621-3630 — Leyland Atlantean PDR1/1 — Metro-Cammell — H44/33F — 1959

3621	UNB621	3623	UNB623	3625	UNB625	3627	UNB627	3629	UNB629
3622	UNB622	3624	UNB624	3626	UNB626	3628	UNB628	3630	UNB630

3631-3670 — Leyland Titan PD2/37 — Metro-Cammell — H37/28R — 1961

3631	9831NA	3639	9839NA	3647	9847NA	3655	9855NA	3663	9863NA
3632	9832NA	3640	9840NA	3648	9848NA	3656	9856NA	3664	9864NA
3633	9833NA	3641	9841NA	3649	9849NA	3657	9857NA	3665	9865NA
3634	9834NA	3642	9842NA	3650	9850NA	3658	9858NA	3666	9866NA
3635	9835NA	3643	9843NA	3651	9851NA	3659	9859NA	3667	9867NA
3636	9836NA	3644	9844NA	3652	9852NA	3660	9860NA	3668	9868NA
3637	9837NA	3645	9845NA	3653	9853NA	3661	9861NA	3669	9869NA
3638	9838NA	3646	9846NA	3654	9854NA	3662	9862NA	3670	9870NA

3671-3695 — Leyland Titan PD2/37 — Metro-Cammell — H37/28R — 1963

3671	3671NE	3676	3676NE	3681	3681NE	3686	3686NE	3691	3691NE
3672	3672NE	3677	3677NE	3682	3682NE	3687	3687NE	3692	3692NE
3673	3673NE	3678	3678NE	3683	3683NE	3688	3688NE	3693	3693NE
3674	3674NE	3679	3679NE	3684	3684NE	3689	3689NE	3694	3694NE
3675	3675NE	3680	3680NE	3685	3685NE	3690	3690NE	3695	3695NE

3696-3720 — Leyland Titan PD2/37 — Metro-Cammell — H37/28R — 1964

3696	889VU	3701	3701VM	3706	3706VM	3711	3711VM	3716	3716VM
3697	3697VM	3702	3702VM	3707	3707VM	3712	3712VM	3717	3717VM
3698	3698VM	3703	3703VM	3708	3708VM	3713	3713VM	3718	3718VM
3699	3699VM	3704	3704VM	3709	3709VM	3714	3714VM	3719	3719VM
3700	3700VM	3705	3705VM	3710	3710VM	3715	3715VM	3720	3720VM

The 1968 North West Bus Handbook

Manchester divided most of its chassis business between Daimler and Leyland. Metro-Cammell bodywork is fitted to 4154, a 1951 CVG6, seen here passing along Portland Street. *Roy Marshall*

3721-3792   Leyland Atlantean PDR1/2   Metro-Cammell   H43/33F   1965

3721	BND721C	3736	BND736C	3751	BND751C	3765	BND765C	3779	BND779C
3722	BND722C	3737	BND737C	3752	BND752C	3766	BND766C	3780	BND780C
3723	BND723C	3738	BND738C	3753	BND753C	3767	BND767C	3781	BND781C
3724	BND724C	3739	BND739C	3754	BND754C	3768	BND768C	3782	BND782C
3725	BND725C	3740	BND740C	3755	BND755C	3769	BND769C	3783	BND783C
3726	BND726C	3741	BND741C	3756	BND756C	3770	BND770C	3784	BND784C
3727	BND727C	3742	BND742C	3757	BND757C	3771	BND771C	3785	BND785C
3728	BND728C	3743	BND743C	3758	BND758C	3772	BND772C	3786	BND786C
3729	BND729C	3744	BND744C	3759	BND759C	3773	BND773C	3787	BND787C
3730	BND730C	3745	BND745C	3760	BND760C	3774	BND774C	3788	BND788C
3731	BND731C	3746	BND746C	3761	BND761C	3775	BND775C	3789	BND789C
3732	BND732C	3747	BND747C	3762	BND762C	3776	BND776C	3790	BND790C
3733	BND733C	3748	BND748C	3763	BND763C	3777	BND777C	3791	BND791C
3734	BND734C	3749	BND749C	3764	BND764C	3778	BND778C	3792	BND792C
3735	BND735C	3750	BND750C						

3801-3860   Leyland Atlantean PDR1/2   Metro-Cammell   H43/33F   1966

3801	END801D	3813	END813D	3825	END825D	3837	END837D	3849	END849D
3802	END802D	3814	END814D	3826	END826D	3838	END838D	3850	END850D
3803	END803D	3815	END815D	3827	END827D	3839	END839D	3851	END851D
3804	END804D	3816	END816D	3828	END828D	3840	END840D	3852	END852D
3805	END805D	3817	END817D	3829	END829D	3841	END841D	3853	END853D
3806	END806D	3818	END818D	3830	END830D	3842	END842D	3854	END854D
3807	END807D	3819	END819D	3831	END831D	3843	END843D	3855	END855D
3808	END808D	3810	END810D	3832	END832D	3844	END844D	3856	END856D
3809	END809D	3821	END821D	3833	END833D	3845	END845D	3857	END857D
3810	END810D	3822	END822D	3834	END834D	3846	END846D	3858	END858D
3811	END811D	3823	END823D	3835	END835D	3847	END847D	3859	END859D
3812	END812D	3824	END824D	3836	END836D	3848	END848D	3860	END860D

4021-4049 — Daimler CVG5 — Crossley — H32/26R — 1949

4021	GVR323	4029	GVR331	4035	GVR337	4039	GVR341	4044	GVR346
4023	GVR325	4030	GVR332	4036	GVR338	4040	GVR342	4047	GVR349
4026	GVR328	4031	GVR333	4037	GVR339	4042	GVR344	4048	GVR350
4027	GVR329	4032	GVR334	4038	GVR340	4043	GVR345	4049	GVR351
4028	GVR330	4033	GVR335						

4051-4099 — Daimler CVG5 — Brush — H32/26R — 1947-48

4051	GVR353	4075	GVR377	4085	GVR387	4090	GVR392	4095	GVR397
4052	GVR354	4076	GVR378	4086	GVR388	4091	GVR393	4096	GVR398
4055	GVR357	4079	GVR381	4087	GVR389	4093	GVR395	4099	GVR401
4056	GVR358	4083	GVR385	4089	GVR391				

4100-4148 — Daimler CVG6 — Metro-Cammell — H32/26R — 1950-51

4100	JND701	4110	JND711	4120	JND721	4130	JND731	4140	JND741
4101	JND702	4111	JND712	4121	JND722	4131	JND732	4141	JND742
4102	JND703	4112	JND713	4122	JND723	4132	JND733	4142	JND743
4103	JND704	4113	JND714	4123	JND724	4133	JND734	4143	JND744
4104	JND705	4114	JND715	4124	JND725	4134	JND735	4144	JND745
4105	JND706	4115	JND716	4125	JND726	4135	JND736	4145	JND746
4106	JND707	4116	JND717	4126	JND727	4136	JND737	4146	JND747
4107	JND708	4117	JND718	4127	JND728	4137	JND738	4147	JND748
4108	JND709	4118	JND719	4128	JND729	4138	JND739	4148	JND749
4109	JND710	4119	JND720	4129	JND730	4139	JND740		

4150-4189 — Daimler CVG6 — Metro-Cammell — H32/26R — 1951

4150	KND911	4158	KND919	4166	KND927	4174	KND935	4182	KND943
4151	KND912	4159	KND920	4167	KND928	4175	KND936	4183	KND944
4152	KND913	4160	KND921	4168	KND929	4176	KND937	4184	KND945
4153	KND914	4161	KND922	4169	KND930	4177	KND938	4185	KND946
4154	KND915	4162	KND923	4170	KND931	4178	KND939	4186	KND947
4155	KND916	4163	KND924	4171	KND932	4179	KND940	4187	KND948
4156	KND917	4164	KND925	4172	KND933	4180	KND941	4188	KND949
4157	KND918	4165	KND926	4173	KND934	4181	KND942	4189	KND950

4400-4489 — Daimler CVG6 — Metro-Cammell — H32/28R — 1953-55 — *4480-89 are H33/28R

4400	NNB210	4418	NNB228	4436	NNB246	4454	NNB264	4472	NNB282
4401	NNB211	4419	NNB229	4437	NNB247	4455	NNB265	4473	NNB283
4402	NNB212	4420	NNB230	4438	NNB248	4456	NNB266	4474	NNB284
4403	NNB213	4421	NNB231	4439	NNB249	4457	NNB267	4475	NNB285
4404	NNB214	4422	NNB232	4440	NNB250	4458	NNB268	4476	NNB286
4405	NNB215	4423	NNB233	4441	NNB251	4459	NNB269	4477	NNB287
4406	NNB216	4424	NNB234	4442	NNB252	4460	NNB270	4478	NNB288
4407	NNB217	4425	NNB235	4443	NNB253	4461	NNB271	4479	NNB289
4408	NNB218	4426	NNB236	4444	NNB254	4462	NNB272	4480	NNB290
4409	NNB219	4427	NNB237	4445	NNB255	4463	NNB273	4481	NNB291
4410	NNB220	4428	NNB238	4446	NNB256	4464	NNB274	4482	NNB292
4411	NNB221	4429	NNB239	4447	NNB257	4465	NNB275	4483	NNB293
4412	NNB222	4430	NNB240	4448	NNB258	4466	NNB276	4484	NNB294
4413	NNB223	4431	NNB241	4449	NNB259	4467	NNB277	4485	NNB295
4414	NNB224	4432	NNB242	4450	NNB260	4468	NNB278	4486	NNB296
4415	NNB225	4433	NNB243	4451	NNB261	4469	NNB279	4487	NNB297
4416	NNB226	4434	NNB244	4452	NNB262	4470	NNB280	4488	NNB298
4417	NNB227	4435	NNB245	4453	NNB263	4471	NNB281	4489	NNB299

4490-4509 — Daimler CVG5* — Metro-Cammell — H36/28R — 1955 — 4490 is CLG5

4490	PND490	4494	PND494	4498	PND498	4502	PND502	4506	PND506
4491	PND491	4495	PND495	4499	PND499	4503	PND503	4507	PND507
4492	PND492	4496	PND496	4500	PND500	4504	PND504	4508	PND508
4493	PND493	4497	PND497	4501	PND501	4505	PND505	4509	PND509

4510-4549   Daimler CVG5   Northern Counties   H37/28R   1956-57

4510	RND510	4518	RND518	4526	RND526	4534	RND534	4542	RND542
4511	RND511	4519	RND519	4527	RND527	4535	RND535	4543	RND543
4512	RND512	4520	RND520	4528	RND528	4536	RND536	4544	RND544
4513	RND513	4521	RND521	4529	RND529	4537	RND537	4545	RND545
4514	RND514	4522	RND522	4530	RND530	4538	RND538	4546	RND546
4515	RND515	4523	RND523	4531	RND531	4539	RND539	4547	RND547
4516	RND516	4524	RND524	4532	RND532	4540	RND540	4548	RND548
4517	RND517	4525	RND525	4533	RND533	4541	RND541	4549	RND549

4550-4579   Daimler CVG5   Burlingham   H37/28R   1957-58

4550	TNA550	4556	TNA556	4562	TNA562	4568	TNA568	4574	TNA574
4551	TNA551	4557	TNA557	4563	TNA563	4569	TNA569	4575	TNA575
4552	TNA552	4558	TNA558	4564	TNA564	4570	TNA570	4576	TNA576
4553	TNA553	4559	TNA559	4565	TNA565	4571	TNA571	4577	TNA577
4554	TNA554	4560	TNA560	4566	TNA566	4572	TNA572	4578	TNA578
4555	TNA555	4561	TNA561	4567	TNA567	4573	TNA573	4579	TNA579

4580-4589   Daimler CVG6   Metro-Cammell   H37/28R   1961

4580	9580NA	4582	9582NA	4584	9584NA	4586	9586NA	4588	9588NA
4581	9581NA	4583	9583NA	4585	9585NA	4587	9587NA	4589	9589NA

4590-4629   Daimler Fleetline CRG6   Metro-Cammell   H43/33F   1962-63

4590	4590NE	4598	4598NE	4606	4606NE	4614	4614VM	4622	4622VM
4591	4591NE	4599	4599NE	4607	4607NE	4615	4615VM	4623	4623VM
4592	4592NE	4600	4600NE	4608	4608NE	4616	4616VM	4624	4624VM
4593	4593NE	4601	4601NE	4609	4609NE	4617	4617VM	4625	4625VM
4594	4594NE	4602	4602NE	4610	4610VM	4618	4618VM	4626	4626VM
4595	4595NE	4603	4603NE	4611	4611VM	4619	4619VM	4627	4627VM
4596	4596NE	4604	4604NE	4612	4612VM	4620	4620VM	4628	4628VM
4597	4597NE	4605	4605NE	4613	4613VM	4621	4621VM	4629	4629VM

4630-4654   Daimler CVG6*   Metro-Cammell   H37/28R   1963   *4650-54 are CCG6

4630	4630VM	4635	4635VM	4640	4640VM	4645	4645VM	4650	4650VM
4631	4631VM	4636	4636VM	4641	4641VM	4646	4646VM	4651	4651VM
4632	4632VM	4637	4637VM	4642	4642VM	4647	4647VM	4652	4652VM
4633	4633VM	4638	4638VM	4643	4643VM	4648	4648VM	4653	4653VM
4634	4634VM	4639	4639VM	4644	4644VM	4649	4649VM	4654	4654VM

4655-4684   Daimler Fleetline CRG6   Metro-Cammell   H43/33F   1964

4655	ANA655B	4661	ANA661B	4667	ANA667B	4673	ANA673B	4679	ANA679B
4656	ANA656B	4662	ANA662B	4668	ANA668B	4674	ANA674B	4680	ANA680B
4657	ANA657B	4663	ANA663B	4669	ANA669B	4675	ANA675B	4681	ANA681B
4658	ANA658B	4664	ANA664B	4670	ANA670B	4676	ANA676B	4682	ANA682B
4659	ANA659B	4665	ANA665B	4671	ANA671B	4677	ANA677B	4683	ANA683B
4660	ANA660B	4666	ANA666B	4672	ANA672B	4678	ANA678B	4684	ANA684B

4701-4760   Daimler Fleetline CRG6LX   Metro-Cammell   H43/33F   1965-67

4701	DNF701C	4713	DNF713C	4725	DNF725C	4737	FNE737D	4749	FNE749D
4702	DNF702C	4714	DNF714C	4726	DNF726C	4738	FNE738D	4750	FNE750D
4703	DNF703C	4715	DNF715C	4727	DNF727C	4739	FNE739D	4751	FNE751D
4704	DNF704C	4716	DNF716C	4728	DNF728C	4740	FNE740D	4752	FNE752D
4705	DNF705C	4717	DNF717C	4729	DNF729C	4741	FNE741D	4753	FNE753D
4706	DNF706C	4718	DNF718C	4730	DNF730C	4742	FNE742D	4754	FNE754D
4707	DNF707C	4719	DNF719C	4731	FNE731D	4743	FNE743D	4755	FNE755D
4708	DNF708C	4720	DNF720C	4732	FNE732D	4744	FNE744D	4756	FNE756D
4709	DNF709C	4721	DNF721C	4733	FNE733D	4745	FNE745D	4757	FNE757D
4710	DNF710C	4722	DNF722C	4734	FNE734D	4746	FNE746D	4758	FNE758D
4711	DNF711C	4723	DNF723C	4735	FNE735D	4747	FNE747D	4759	FNE759D
4712	DNF712C	4724	DNF724C	4736	FNE736D	4748	FNE748D	4760	FNE760D

Livery: Red and white

MORECAMBE & HEYSHAM

Morecambe & Heysham Corporation Transport Department, Heysham Road, Morecambe.

Morecambe Corporation became a tramway operator in 1909, taking over a line owned by the corporation but operated by the Morecambe Tramways Company. When this closed in 1926 it was the last horse tramway on the British mainland.

Bus operation started in 1919 with double-deckers, six-wheel Guys, being introduced at the relatively early date of 1926. The new borough of Morecambe & Heysham was created in 1928, and in the following year it purchased Heysham & District Motors, which dated from 1924 and had taken over the bus operations of Morecambe Tramways.

For three decades from the early 1930s all new buses were AECs with petrol engines, which gave Morecambe & Heysham the distinction of being the last operator of petrol-engined double-deckers in Britain, when the final petrol-engined Regent was withdrawn in 1959.

The future: When local government was reorganised in 1974, Morecambe & Heysham's bus operations were absorbed by Lancaster City Transport.

1-7			AEC Swift MP2R		Pennine		B50D	1967-68		
1	CTJ101E	3	CTJ103E	5	CTJ105E	6	CTJ106E	7	HTF377F	
2	CTJ102E	4	CTJ104E							

18-23			AEC Regent III 6811A		Park Royal		H30/26R	1948		
18	JTE544	20	JTE546	21	JTE547	22	JTE548	23	JTE549	
19	JTE545									

AEC was the major chassis supplier to Morecambe & Heysham. The undertaking's last Regents were five Mark V models with Massey bodies, delivered in 1957.
Reg Wilson

In 1967 Morecambe & Heysham introduced one-man-operation using a fleet of AEC Swifts with bodywork by Pennine, more commonly associated with Seddon chassis. Pennine, based in Oldham, was owned by Seddon. *Michael Fowler*

54-71

| | | AEC Regent III 9612E | | Park Royal | | H33/26R* | 1949-50 | *60-65 are O33/26R |

54	KTF583	58	KTF587	62	KTF591	66	LTF251	69	LTF254
55	KTF584	59	KTF588	63	KTF592	67	LTF252	70	LTF255
56	KTF585	60	KTF589	64	KTF593	68	LTF253	71	LTF256
57	KTF586	61	KTF590	65	KTF594				

| 72 | MTC540 | AEC Regent III 9613E | Park Royal | H33/26R | 1950 |

73-78

| | | AEC Regent III 6812A | | Weymann | | H33/26R | 1951 | |

| 73 | MTE635 | 75 | MTE637 | 76 | MTE638 | 77 | MTE639 | 78 | MTE640 |
| 74 | MTE636 | | | | | | | | |

79	TTB688	AEC Regent III 6812A	Park Royal	H33/26R	1954
80	TTB689	AEC Regent III 6812A	Park Royal	H33/26R	1954
81	TTB690	AEC Regent III 6812A	Park Royal	H33/26R	1954

82-86

| | | AEC Regent V MD3RV | | Massey | | H33/26R | 1957 | |

| 82 | 791ATD | 83 | 792ATD | 84 | 793ATD | 85 | 794ATD | 86 | 795ATD |

87	33MTD	Leyland Titan PD2/37	Massey	H37/27F	1960
88	34MTD	Leyland Titan PD2/37	Massey	H37/27F	1960
89	35MTD	Leyland Titan PD2/37	Massey	H37/27F	1960
90	435XTF	Leyland Titan PD2A/27	Massey	H37/27F	1962
91	436XTF	Leyland Titan PD2A/27	Massey	H37/27F	1962

Livery: Green and cream

The 1968 North West Bus Handbook

NORTH WESTERN

North Western Road Car Company, Charles Street, Stockport

The North Western Road Car Co was created in 1923, taking over an operation started by the British Automobile Traction Co ten years earlier. It was owned jointly by Tilling and BAT, and in 1928 became a subsidiary of the newly-created Tilling and British Automobile Traction group. When TBAT was split in 1942 ownership went to BET.

Bristols featured in the fleet for many years, and when that make ceased to be available on the open market the bulk of North Western's orders went to AEC and Leyland.

Subsidiary companies included Altrincham Coachways and Melba Motors, both acquired in 1958 and operated under their own identities until 1967.

The future: Some 60 per cent of North Western's route mileage was in the area of the SELNEC PTE, created in 1969. In 1972 that part of the company's operations was sold to SELNEC, with the remaining routes being shared between Crosville and Trent - which, like North Western, were by that time part of NBC. The company's coaching fleet formed a key part of the new National Travel (North West) business created in 1973. The North Western name then disappeared - but was revived in 1986 for a new company created by NBC to take over the southern part of Ribble's operations in the run up to privatisation.

There were two batches of AEC Renowns with Park Royal bodies in the North Western fleet. Although it operated a large fleet of Reliances, these were the only double-deckers supplied by AEC in postwar years.
Roy Marshall

1-21
Daimler Fleetline CRG6LX — Alexander D — H44/31F — 1963

1	YJA1	5	YJA5	10	YJA10	14	YJA14	18	YJA18
2	YJA2	6	YJA6	11	YJA11	15	YJA15	19	YJA19
3	YJA3	8	YJA8	12	YJA12	16	YJA16	20	YJA21
4	YJA4	9	YJA9	13	YJA13	17	YJA17	21	YJA21

100-114
Daimler Fleetline CRG6LX — Alexander D — H44/31F — 1964

100	AJA100B	103	AJA103B	106	AJA106B	109	AJA109B	112	AJA112B
101	AJA101B	104	AJA104B	107	AJA107B	110	AJA110B	113	AJA113B
102	AJA102B	105	AJA105B	108	AJA108B	111	AJA111B	114	AJA114B

115-129
AEC Renown 3B3RA — Park Royal — H42/30F — 1964

115	AJA115B	118	AJA118B	121	AJA121B	124	AJA124B	127	AJA127B
116	AJA116B	119	AJA119B	122	AJA122B	125	AJA125B	128	AJA128B
117	AJA117B	120	AJA120B	123	AJA123B	126	AJA126B	129	AJA129B

130-139
Bedford VAL14 — Strachan — B52F — 1964

130	AJA130B	132	AJA132B	134	AJA134B	136	AJA136B	138	AJA138B
131	AJA131B	133	AJA133B	135	AJA135B	137	AJA137B	139	AJA139B

140-149
Leyland Leopard PSU3/3RT — Alexander Y — C49F — 1964

140	AJA140B	142	AJA142B	144	AJA144B	146	AJA146B	148	AJA148B
141	AJA141B	143	AJA143B	145	AJA145B	147	AJA147B	149	AJA149B

150-154
Leyland Leopard L2T — Harrington Grenadier — C41F — 1964-65

150	AJA150B	151	AJA151B	152	DDB152C	153	DDB153C	154	DDB154C

155-164
Leyland Leopard PSU3/3RT — Alexander Y — C49F — 1965

155	DDB155C	158	DDB158C	160	DDB160C	162	DDB162C	164	DDB164C
156	DDB156C	159	DDB159C	161	DDB161C	163	DDB163C	165	DDB165C
157	DDB157C								

165-188
Daimler Fleetline CRG6LX — Alexander D — H44/31F — 1965-66

165	DDB165C	170	DDB170C	175	DDB175C	180	DDB180C	185	DDB185C
166	DDB166C	171	DDB171C	176	DDB176C	181	DDB181C	186	DDB186C
167	DDB167C	172	DDB172C	177	DDB177C	182	DDB182C	187	DDB187C
168	DDB168C	173	DDB173C	178	DDB178C	183	DDB183C	188	DDB188C
169	DDB169C	174	DDB174C	179	DDB179C	184	DDB184C		

189	DDB189C	Daimler Fleetline CRC6	Alexander D	H44/31F	1965

North Western chose Alexander-bodied low-height Fleetlines for their new generation double-deck needs, most being allocated at depots in the south Manchester conurbation.
Roy Marshall

190-214

Daimler Fleetline CRG6LX Alexander D H44/31F 1966

190	FJA190D	195	FJA195D	200	FJA200D	205	FJA205D	210	FJA210D
191	FJA191D	196	FJA196D	201	FJA201D	206	FJA206D	211	FJA211D
192	FJA192D	197	FJA197D	202	FJA202D	207	FJA207D	212	FJA212D
193	FJA193D	198	FJA198D	203	FJA203D	208	FJA208D	213	FJA213D
194	FJA194D	199	FJA199D	204	FJA204D	209	FJA209D	214	FJA214D

215-224

Leyland Leopard PSU3/4R Alexander Y C49F 1966

215	FJA215D	217	FJA217D	219	FJA219D	221	FJA221D	223	FJA223D
216	FJA216D	218	FJA218D	220	FJA220D	222	FJA222D	224	FJA224D

225-234

Leyland Leopard PSU4/4R Duple Commander C41F 1966-67

225	FJA225D	227	FJA227D	229	FJA229D	221	JDB231E	233	JDB233E
216	FJA226D	228	FJA228D	230	JDB230E	232	JDB232E	234	JDB234E

235-244

Leyland Leopard PSU3/4R Alexander Y C49F 1967

235	JDB235E	237	JDB237E	239	JDB239E	241	JDB241E	243	JDB243E
236	JDB236E	238	JDB238E	240	JDB240E	242	JDB242E	244	JDB244E

245-254

Daimler Fleetline CRG6LX Alexander D H44/31F 1967

245	JDB245F	247	JDB247F	249	JDB249F	251	JDB251F	253	JDB253F
246	JDB246F	248	JDB248F	250	JDB250F	252	JDB252F	254	JDB254F

255-259

Leyland Leopard PSU4/4R Duple Commander C41F* 1968 *259 is C37F

255	KJA255F	256	KJA256F	257	KJA257F	258	KJA258F	259	KJA259F

260-269

Leyland Leopard PSU3/4R Alexander Y C49F 1968

260	KJA260F	262	KJA262F	264	KJA264F	266	KJA266F	268	KJA268F
261	KJA261F	263	KJA263F	265	KJA265F	267	KJA267F	269	KJA269F

270-309

Bristol RESL6G Marshall B45F 1968

270	KJA270F	278	KJA278F	286	KJA286F	294	KJA294G	302	KJA302G
271	KJA271F	279	KJA279F	287	KJA287F	295	KJA295G	303	KJA303G
272	KJA272F	280	KJA280F	288	KJA288F	296	KJA296G	304	KJA304G
273	KJA273F	281	KJA281F	289	KJA289F	297	KJA297G	305	KJA305G
274	KJA274F	282	KJA282F	290	KJA290F	298	KJA298G	306	KJA306G
275	KJA275F	283	KJA283F	291	KJA291G	299	KJA299G	307	KJA307G
276	KJA276F	284	KJA284F	292	KJA292G	300	KJA300G	308	KJA308G
277	KJA277F	285	KJA285F	293	KJA293G	301	KJA301G	309	KJA309G

517-549

Leyland Royal Tiger PSU1/13 Weymann B44F 1953

517	FDB517	523	FDB523	527	FDB527	543	FDB543	547	FDB547
520	FDB520	524	FDB524	528	FDB528	545	FDB545	548	FDB548
521	FDB521	525	FDB525	529	FDB529	546	FDB546	549	FDB549
522	FDB522	526	FDB526						

556	FDB556	AEC Reliance MU3RA	Weymann	B44F	1954
557	FDB557	AEC Reliance MU3RA	Weymann	B44F	1954
558	FDB558	AEC Reliance MU3RA	Weymann	B44F	1954
559	FDB559	AEC Reliance MU3RA	Weymann	B44F	1954

Opposite, top: **When North Western's fleet numbers reached 981 in 1963 it reverted to 1 for its next intake of buses - 21 Fleetlines - to avoid taking numbers above 999. The Stockport licensing office normally issued two-figure numbers to motorcycles, and in 1964 a new series commenced at 100, to ensure the availability of matching registrations, a feature of the North Western fleet since 1946. Some of the 1964 Renowns, including 128. were fitted with seats with higher than normal backs, removed from a batch of AEC Reliances.** *Reg Wilson*

Opposite, bottom: **Having been a major user of Bristols prior to that manufacturer coming under state control, North Western was among the companies which were quick to buy Bristols when they again became available on the open market. In 1968 it took 40 RESL6G models with 45-seat Marshall bodies. When buses were equipped for pay as you board an 'A' suffix was applied to the fleet number.** *Reg Wilson*

Alexander became a major supplier to North Western in the early 1960s. This multi-windowed 36ft-long body style was unique to North Western and was in essence a lengthened version of an existing Alexander body. Ten, on Leyland Leopard chassis, were supplied in 1962. From 1963 the Y-type would be the standard Alexander single-deck body for mid-engined chassis, and North Western would be among the users.
Roy Marshall

560-596   Leyland Tiger Cub PSUC1/1   Weymann   B44F   1954-55

560	FDB560	577	FDB577	582	FDB582	587	FDB587	592	FDB592
561	FDB561	578	FDB578	583	FDB583	588	FDB588	593	FDB593
562	FDB562	579	FDB579	584	FDB584	589	FDB589	594	FDB594
563	FDB563	580	FDB580	585	FDB585	590	FDB590	595	FDB595
564	FDB564	581	FDB581	586	FDB586	591	FDB591	596	FDB596

631-660   Leyland Tiger Cub PSUC1/1   Weymann   B44F   1956

631	KDB631	637	KDB637	643	KDB643	649	KDB649	655	KDB655
632	KDB632	638	KDB638	644	KDB644	650	KDB650	656	KDB656
633	KDB633	639	KDB639	645	KDB645	651	KDB651	657	KDB657
634	KDB634	640	KDB640	646	KDB646	652	KDB652	658	KDB658
635	KDB635	641	KDB641	647	KDB647	653	KDB653	659	KDB659
636	KDB636	642	KDB642	648	KDB648	654	KDB654	660	KDB660

661-670   Leyland Titan PD2/21   Weymann   L30/28RD   1956

661	KDB661	663	KDB663	665	KDB665	667	KDB667	669	KDB669
662	KDB662	664	KDB664	666	KDB666	668	KDB668	670	KDB670

671-700   Leyland Tiger Cub PSUC1/1   Weymann   B44F   1957

671	KDB671	677	KDB677	683	KDB683	689	KDB689	695	KDB695
672	KDB672	678	KDB678	684	KDB684	690	KDB690	696	KDB696
673	KDB673	679	KDB679	685	KDB685	691	KDB691	697	KDB697
674	KDB674	680	KDB680	686	KDB686	692	KDB692	698	KDB698
675	KDB675	681	KDB681	687	KDB687	693	KDB693	699	KDB699
676	KDB676	682	KDB682	688	KDB688	694	KDB694	700	KDB700

713	LDB713	AEC Reliance MU3RA	Burlingham Seagull	C41C	1956

North Western reserved blocks of 100 registrations at a time, with LDB701-800 covering the period from 1956 to 1960. In 1958 it added six Reliances to its coach fleet with unusual Weymann Fanfare bodywork, at which time it was half way through the LDB registration series. *Roy Marshall*

720-739

AEC Reliance MU3RA   Weymann   DP43F   1957

720	LDB720	724	LDB724	728	LDB728	732	LDB732	736	LDB736
721	LDB721	725	LDB725	729	LDB729	733	LDB733	737	LDB737
722	LDB722	726	LDB726	730	LDB730	734	LDB734	738	LDB738
723	LDB723	727	LDB727	731	LDB731	735	LDB735	739	LDB739

740-745

AEC Reliance MU3RA   Weymann Fanfare   C41F   1958

740	LDB740	742	LDB742	743	LDB743	744	LDB744	745	LDB745
741	LDB741								

746-760

AEC Reliance MU3RA   Willowbrook   DP43F   1958

746	LDB746	749	LDB749	752	LDB752	755	LDB755	758	LDB758
747	LDB747	750	LDB750	753	LDB753	756	LDB756	759	LDB759
748	LDB748	751	LDB751	754	LDB754	757	LDB757	760	LDB760

761-765

Leyland Tiger Cub PSUC1/2   Willowbrook   DP43F   1958

761	LDB761	762	LDB762	763	LDB763	764	LDB764	765	LDB765

766-775

Leyland Tiger Cub PSUC1/2T   Willowbrook   DP41F   1958

766	LDB766	768	LDB768	770	LDB770	772	LDB772	774	LDB774
767	LDB767	769	LDB769	771	LDB771	773	LDB773	775	LDB775

776-781

AEC Reliance 2MU3RA   Harrington Contender   C41F*   1958   *781 is C37F

776	LDB776	778	LDB778	779	LDB779	780	LDB780	781	LDB781
777	LDB777								

783-796

Leyland Tiger Cub PSUC1/2   Willowbrook   DP43F   1960

783	LDB783	786	LDB786	789	LDB789	792	LDB792	795	LDB795
784	LDB784	787	LDB787	790	LDB790	793	LDB793	796	LDB796
785	LDB785	788	LDB788	791	LDB791	794	LDB794		

797-811   AEC Reliance 2MU3RA   Willowbrook   DP43F   1960

797	LDB797	800	LDB800	803	RDB803	806	RDB806	809	RDB809
798	LDB798	801	RDB801	804	RDB804	807	RDB807	810	RDB810
799	LDB799	802	RDB802	805	RDB805	808	RDB808	811	RDB811

812-826   Dennis Loline   East Lancashire   H39/32F   1960

812	RDB812	815	RDB815	818	RDB818	821	RDB821	824	RDB824
813	RDB813	816	RDB816	819	RDB819	822	RDB822	825	RDB825
814	RDB814	817	RDB817	820	RDB820	823	RDB823	826	RDB826

827-831   AEC Reliance 2MU3RA   Willowbrook Viking   C41F   1960

827	RDB827	828	RDB828	829	RDB829	830	RDB830	831	RDB831

832-851   AEC Reliance 2MU3RA   Alexander Z   C41F   1961

832	RDB832	836	RDB836	840	RDB840	844	RDB844	848	RDB848
833	RDB833	837	RDB837	841	RDB841	845	RDB845	849	RDB849
834	RDB834	838	RDB838	842	RDB842	846	RDB846	850	RDB850
835	RDB835	839	RDB839	843	RDB843	847	RDB847	851	RDB851

852-871   AEC Reliance 2MU3RA   Willowbrook   DP43F   1961

852	RDB852	856	RDB856	860	RDB860	864	RDB864	868	RDB868
853	RDB853	857	RDB857	861	RDB861	865	RDB865	869	RDB869
854	RDB854	858	RDB858	862	RDB862	866	RDB866	870	RDB870
855	RDB855	859	RDB859	863	RDB863	867	RDB867	871	RDB871

872-906   Dennis Loline III   Alexander G   H39/32F   1961-62

872	RDB872	879	RDB879	886	RDB886	893	RDB893	900	RDB900
873	RDB873	880	RDB880	887	RDB887	894	RDB894	901	VDB901
874	RDB874	881	RDB881	888	RDB888	895	RDB895	902	VDB902
875	RDB875	882	RDB882	889	RDB889	896	RDB896	903	VDB903
876	RDB876	883	RDB883	890	RDB890	897	RDB897	904	VDB904
877	RDB877	884	RDB884	891	RDB891	898	RDB898	905	VDB905
878	RDB878	885	RDB885	892	RDB892	899	RDB899	906	VDB906

907-916   Leyland Leopard PSU3/3RT   Alexander Z   C49F   1962

907	VDB907	909	VDB909	911	VDB911	913	VDB913	915	VDB915
908	VDB908	910	VDB910	912	VDB912	914	VDB914	916	VDB916

917-951   AEC Reliance 2MU3RA   Willowbrook   B53F*   1963   *932-51 are DP51F

917	VDB917	924	VDB924	931	VDB931	938	VDB938	945	VDB945
918	VDB918	925	VDB925	932	VDB932	939	VDB939	946	VDB946
919	VDB919	926	VDB926	933	VDB933	940	VDB940	947	VDB947
920	VDB920	927	VDB927	934	VDB934	941	VDB941	948	VDB948
921	VDB921	928	VDB928	935	VDB935	942	VDB942	949	VDB949
922	VDB922	929	VDB929	936	VDB936	943	VDB943	950	VDB950
923	VDB923	930	VDB930	937	VDB937	944	VDB944	951	VDB951

952-961   Leyland Leopard PSU3/3RT   Alexander Y   C49F   1963

952	VDB952	954	VDB954	956	VDB956	958	VDB958	960	VDB960
953	VDB953	955	VDB955	957	VDB957	959	VDB959	961	VDB961

962	VDB962	Leyland Leopard PSU3/3RT	Plaxton Panorama	C49F	1963
963	VDB963	Leyland Leopard PSU3/3RT	Plaxton Panorama	C49F	1963

964-981   AEC Renown 3B3RA   Park Royal   H42/32F   1963

964	VDB964	968	VDB968	972	VDB972	976	VDB976	979	VDB979
965	VDB965	969	VDB969	973	VDB973	977	VDB977	980	VDB980
966	VDB966	970	VDB970	974	VDB974	978	VDB978	981	VDB981
967	VDB967	971	VDB971	975	VDB975				

Livery: Red and cream, dual-purpose with added black.

OLDHAM

Oldham Corporation Transport Department, Walshaw Street, Oldham

In 1901 Oldham Corporation started running electric trams, replacing two company-owned services. It operated trams until 1946. Buses were tried experimentally from 1913, and included an unusual battery-electric vehicle. Operations ceased in 1919, then restarted on a permanent basis at the end of 1924. Two trolleybuses joined the fleet in 1925, for operation on a joint service with Ashton-under-Lyne, which bought eight similar vehicles at the same time. Oldham's two trolleys only lasted 12 months.

Three-axle Guys and Karriers were bought in the late 1920s - there were 39 in all - and included double-deckers with remarkably high seating capacity for the time, up to 72 on one Guy. Most new buses in the 1930s were Leylands, and Leyland remained Oldham's main supplier, although a number of Daimlers and Crossleys were purchased in the late 1940s.

In 1944 Oldham (along with Manchester and Rochdale) took over the services between Manchester and Rochdale which were operated by Yelloway Motor Services, a company better known for its express coach operations.

In 1965 Oldham had trouble with vehicle maintenance and to cover shortages it both hired and bought serviceable - but elderly - vehicles from other fleets, most of which were still in service in 1968.

The future: Oldham's bus operations were taken over by the SELNEC PTE in November 1969.

101-110		Leyland Titan PD3/5		Roe		H41/32F	1964		
101	101HBU	**103**	103HBU	**105**	105HBU	**107**	107HBU	**110**	110HBU
102	102HBU	**104**	104HBU	**106**	106HBU	**109**	109HBU		

111	111JBU	Leyland Tiger Cub PSUC1/13	Marshall	B41D	1964
112	112JBU	Leyland Tiger Cub PSUC1/13	Marshall	B41D	1964
113	113JBU	Leyland Tiger Cub PSUC1/13	Marshall	B41D	1964
114	114JBU	Leyland Tiger Cub PSUC1/13	Marshall	B41D	1964
115	115JBU	Leyland Tiger Cub PSUC1/13	Pennine	B41D	1965
116	116JBU	Leyland Tiger Cub PSUC1/13	Pennine	B41D	1965
117	LBU117E	Leyland Panther Cub PSRC1/1	Marshall	B45D	1967
118	LBU118E	Leyland Panther Cub PSRC1/1	Marshall	B45D	1967
119	LBU119E	Leyland Panther Cub PSRC1/1	Marshall	B45D	1967
120	LBU120E	Leyland Panther Cub PSRC1/1	Marshall	B45D	1967

121-130		Leyland Atlantean PDR1/2		Roe		H43/34F	1965		
121	CBU121C	**123**	CBU123C	**125**	CBU125C	**127**	CBU127C	**129**	CBU129C
122	CBU122C	**124**	CBU124C	**126**	CBU126C	**128**	CBU128C	**130**	CBU130C

131-135		Leyland Atlantean PDR1/1		East Lancashire		H43/34F	1966		
131	GBU131D	**132**	GBU132D	**133**	GBU133D	**134**	GBU134D	**135**	GBU135D

Oldham's long-standing bodywork supplier, Roe, provided the bodywork for the first ten new generation double-deck buses that arrived in 1965. *Roy Marshall*

136-147

							Leyland Atlantean PDR1/1		Roe			H43/34F	1966	
136	GBU136D	**139**	GBU139D	**142**	GBU142D	**144**	GBU144D	**146**	GBU146D
137	GBU137D	**140**	GBU140D	**143**	GBU143D	**145**	GBU145D	**147**	GBU147D
138	GBU138D	**141**	GBU141D						

148-152

				Leyland Atlantean PDR1/1		Neepsend				H43/34F	1967	
148	LBU148E	**149**	LBU149E	**150**	LBU150E	**151**	LBU151E	**152**	LBU152E

153-171

							Leyland Atlantean PDR1/1		Roe			H43/34F	1967	
153	LBU153E	**157**	LBU157E	**161**	OBU161F	**165**	OBU165F	**169**	OBU169F
154	LBU154E	**158**	LBU158E	**162**	OBU162F	**166**	OBU166F	**170**	OBU170F
155	LBU155E	**159**	LBU159E	**163**	OBU163F	**167**	OBU167F	**171**	OBU171F
156	LBU156E	**160**	LBU160E	**164**	OBU164F	**168**	OBU168F		

172-177

				Leyland Panther PSUR1/1		Marshall				B49F	1968	
172	OBU172F	**174**	OBU174F	**175**	OBU175F	**176**	OBU176F	**177**	OBU177F
173	OBU173F								

242-291

				Leyland Titan PD1/3		Roe				H31/25R	1947-48	
246	DBU246	**272**	DBU272	**277**	DBU277	**285**	DBU285	**289**	DBU289
262	DBU262	**273**	DBU273	**284**	DBU284	**288**	DBU288	**291**	DBU291
270	DBU270	**275**	DBU275						

Opposite, top: **Oldham experimented with single-deck operation from the mid 1960s when six Leyland Tiger Cubs were delivered from two bodybuilders. These were followed, in 1967, by four Marshall-bodied Panther Cubs. Six Panthers arrived in 1968 and these, too, carried Marshall bodies. Pictured near the college is 174 which illustrates the use of fleet number plates rather than transfers.** *Bill Potter*
Opposite, bottom: **The changing face of Oldham's buses represented by two Roe-bodied Leylands. On the left is a 1966 Atlantean and on the right a 1957 PD2. That just nine years separates the two vehicles illustrates the pace of change at the time.** *Reg Wilson*

338-361   Leyland Titan PD2/3   Roe   H31/25R   1948-50

338	EBU868	343	EBU873	348	EBU878	353	FBU640	358	FBU645
339	EBU869	344	EBU874	349	EBU879	354	FBU641	359	FBU646
340	EBU870	345	EBU875	350	EBU880	355	FBU642	360	FBU647
341	EBU871	346	EBU876	351	EBU881	356	FBU643	361	FBU648
342	EBU872	347	EBU877	352	FBU639	357	FBU644		

370	HBU123	Leyland Titan PD2/12	Leyland	H30/26R	1952
371	HBU124	Leyland Titan PD2/12	Leyland	H30/26R	1952
372	HBU125	Leyland Titan PD2/12	Leyland	H30/26R	1952

373-377   Leyland Titan PD2/20   Metro-Cammell   H30/26R   1955

373	KBU383	374	KBU384	375	KBU385	376	KBU386	377	KBU387

378-387   Leyland Titan PD2/20   Roe   H31/25R   1954-55

378	KBU373	380	KBU375	382	KBU377	384	KBU379	386	KBU381
379	KBU374	381	KBU376	383	KBU378	385	KBU380	387	KBU382

388-407   Leyland Titan PD2/20   Roe   H33/27R   1957

388	NBU488	392	NBU492	396	NBU496	400	NBU500	404	NBU504
389	NBU489	393	NBU493	397	NBU497	401	NBU501	405	NBU505
390	NBU490	394	NBU494	398	NBU498	402	NBU502	406	NBU506
391	NBU491	395	NBU495	399	NBU499	403	NBU503	407	NBU507

408-412   Leyland Titan PD2/20   Crossley   H33/28R   1957

408	NBU508	409	NBU509	410	NBU510	411	NBU511	412	NBU512

413-418   Leyland Titan PD2/20   Northen Counties   H33/28R   1957

413	NBU513	415	NBU515	416	NBU516	417	NBU517	418	NBU518
414	NBU514								

419-428   Leyland Titan PD2/30   Metro-Cammell   H37/28R   1958-59

419	PBU919	421	PBU921	423	PBU923	425	PBU925	427	PBU927
420	PBU920	422	PBU922	424	PBU924	426	PBU926	428	PBU928

429-452   Leyland Titan PD2/30   Roe   H33/28R   1958

429	PBU929	434	PBU934	439	PBU939	444	PBU944	449	PBU949
430	PBU930	435	PBU935	440	PBU940	445	PBU945	450	PBU950
431	PBU931	436	PBU936	441	PBU941	446	PBU946	451	PBU951
432	PBU932	437	PBU937	442	PBU942	447	PBU947	452	PBU952
433	PBU933	438	PBU938	443	PBU943	448	PBU948		

453-462   Leyland Titan PD2/30   Northen Counties   H33/28R   1958-59

453	PBU953	455	PBU955	457	PBU957	459	PBU959	461	PBU961
454	PBU954	456	PBU956	458	PBU958	460	PBU960	462	PBU962

463	LWE104	Leyland Titan PD2/1	Leyland	H33/26R	1949	Sheffield Corporation, 1965
464	LWE109	Leyland Titan PD2/1	Leyland	H30/26R	1949	Sheffield Corporation, 1965
465	LWE110	Leyland Titan PD2/1	Leyland	H30/26R	1949	Sheffield Corporation, 1965
466	LWE111	Leyland Titan PD2/1	Leyland	H30/26R	1949	Sheffield Corporation, 1965
467	ACP392	Leyland Titan PD2/1	Leyland	H33/26R	1948	Halifax Corporation, 1965
468	ACP385	Leyland Titan PD2/1	Leyland	H33/26R	1947	Halifax Corporation, 1965
469	ACP388	Leyland Titan PD2/1	Leyland	H33/26R	1947	Halifax Corporation, 1965
470	ACP390	Leyland Titan PD2/1	Leyland	H33/26R	1947	Halifax Corporation, 1965
471	DBN329	Leyland Titan PD2/4	Leyland	H30/26R	1949	Bolton Corporation, 1965
472	DBN330	Leyland Titan PD2/4	Leyland	H30/26R	1949	Bolton Corporation, 1965
473	DBN337	Leyland Titan PD2/4	Leyland	H30/26R	1949	Bolton Corporation, 1965
474	DBN341	Leyland Titan PD2/4	Leyland	H30/26R	1949	Bolton Corporation, 1965
475	OWB856	Leyland Titan PD2/10	Leyland	H33/28R	1952	Sheffield Corporation, 1965
476	OWB857	Leyland Titan PD2/10	Leyland	H33/28R	1952	Sheffield Corporation, 1965
477	OWB859	Leyland Titan PD2/10	Leyland	H33/28R	1952	Sheffield Corporation, 1965
478	OWB861	Leyland Titan PD2/10	Leyland	H33/28R	1952	Sheffield Corporation, 1965

Livery: Crimson lake and white

PRESTON

Preston Corporation Transport Department, Deepdale Road, Preston

Preston Corporation took over operation of the town's tram services in 1904, electrifying them at the same time. At its peak the tram fleet numbered 48. The system closed in 1935.

Bus operation started in 1922 using three Leylands to provide feeder services to the trams. By 1929 there were 20 buses in the fleet - all Leylands and including five double-deckers. Leylands, mainly Titans, became the Preston standard. The last new Titans joined the fleet in 1965, although thanks to a programme of building "new" PD3s from old PD2s the last Preston Titan, a rebuild, did not enter service until 1967. Preston supported local bodybuilders English Electric and Leyland, only switching to other suppliers when these builders' products had ceased to be available.

There was joint operation of some services with Ribble from 1931. Preston was unusual in using route letters rather than numbers. The letters indicated the outer terminus of the route - eg FP for Farrington Park.

A significant change in policy saw 15 Panthers join the fleet in 1968, at a time when the only other single-deckers were a pair of PS1 Tigers. These were the first new buses to be delivered in the cream and blue colour scheme adopted in 1967 to replace the drab dark maroon previously used.

The future: The operation became Preston Borough Transport in 1974 and was set-up as a council-owned limited company in 1986 to meet the requirements of the 1985 Transport Act. It was sold to its management and employees in 1993, becoming Preston Bus.

2	PRN761		Leyland Titan PD3/6 rebuild	Leyland/PCT		H38/32F	1961	Rebuilt from PD2 (ECK509)
5	NCK757		Leyland Titan PD3/6 rebuild	Leyland/PCT		H38/32F	1960	Rebuilt from PD2 (ECK510)
9	NCK741		Leyland Titan PD3/6 rebuild	Leyland/PCT		H38/32F	1959	Rebuilt from PD2 (FRN731)
10	PRN762		Leyland Titan PD3/6 rebuild	Leyland/PCT		H38/32F	1962	Rebuilt from PD2 (FRN732)

13-19			Leyland Titan PD3/4	Metro-Cammell		H39/31F	1961	
13	PRN905	15	PRN907	17	PRN909	18	PRN910	19	PRN911
14	PRN906	16	PRN908					

20-37			Leyland Titan PD2/10	Crossley		H32/29R	1956-57	*24-9/31-7 are H33/29R
20	KCK328	24	JCK583	28	JCK587	32	KRN423	35	KRN426
21	KCK329	25	JCK584	29	KRN420	33	KRN424	36	KRN427
22	KCK330	26	JCK585	30	KRN421	34	KRN425	37	KRN428
23	KRN419	27	JCK586	31	KRN422			

41-49			Leyland Titan PD2/10	Leyland		H32/29R	1952-54	
41	ECK501	43	ECK503	45	ECK505	47	ECK507	49	FRN733
42	ECK502	44	ECK504	46	ECK506	48	ECK508		

50	SRN375	Leyland Titan PD3/6 rebuild	Leyland/PCT	H38/32F	1963	Rebuilt from PD2 (FRN734)
51	SRN376	Leyland Titan PD3/6 rebuild	Leyland/PCT	H38/32F	1963	Rebuilt from PD2 (FRN735)
53	FRN736	Leyland Titan PD2/10	Leyland	H32/29R	1954	
54	FRN737	Leyland Titan PD2/10	Leyland	H32/29R	1954	
57	FRN738	Leyland Titan PD2/10	Leyland	H32/29R	1954	
59	FCK453F	Leyland Titan PD3/6 rebuild	Leyland/PCT	H38/32F	1967	Rebuilt from PD2 (FRN739)
61	BCK367C	Leyland Titan PD3/6 rebuild	Leyland/PCT	H38/32F	1965	Rebuilt from PD2 (FRN740)

62-68

Leyland Titan PD3/5 — Metro-Cammell — H40/32F — 1958

62	MCK293	64	MCK295	66	MCK297	67	MCK298	68	MCK299
63	MCK294	65	MCK296						

69-73

Leyland Titan PD3A/1 — Metro-Cammell — H39/31F — 1965

69	ARN654C	70	ARN655C	71	ARN656C	72	ARN657C	73	ARN658C

74	CRN79	Leyland Tiger PS1	East Lancashire	B35R	1949
75	CRN80	Leyland Tiger PS1	East Lancashire	B35R	1949

79-83

Leyland Titan PD2/10 — Metro-Cammell — H33/29R — 1955

79	HRN485	80	HRN486	81	HRN487	82	HRN488	83	HRN489

84-90

Leyland Titan PD3A/1 — Metro-Cammell — H39/31F — 1963

84	TRN386	86	TRN388	88	TRN390	89	TRN391	90	TRN392
85	TRN387	87	TRN389						

91	BCK625	Leyland Titan PD1A	Leyland	H32/27R	1947
92	BCK626	Leyland Titan PD1A	Leyland	H30/26R	1947
93	BCK627	Leyland Titan PD1A	Leyland	H30/26R	1947
94	BCK628	Leyland Titan PD1A	Leyland	H30/26R	1947
97	BCK631	Leyland Titan PD1A	Samlesbury	H30/26R	1947

108-127

Leyland Titan PD2/1 — Leyland Farington — H30/26R — 1950-51

108	DRN291	112	DRN295	116	DRN299	120	DRN303	124	DRN307
109	DRN292	113	DRN296	117	DRN300	121	DRN304	125	DRN308
110	DRN293	114	DRN297	118	DRN301	122	DRN305	126	DRN309
111	DRN294	115	DRN298	119	DRN302	123	DRN306	127	DRN310

201-205

Leyland Panther PSUR1A/1 — Metro-Cammell — B47D — 1968

201	HCK201G	202	HCK202G	203	HCK203G	204	HCK204G	205	HCK205G

206-215

Leyland Panther PSUR1A/1 — Marshall — B47D — 1968

206	HCK206G	208	HCK208G	210	HCK210G	212	HCK212G	214	HCK214G
207	HCK207G	209	HCK209G	211	HCK211G	213	HCK213G	215	HCK215G

Livery: Blue and ivory replacing crimson and cream from 1967

Opposite, top: **In changing its livery from maroon to blue Preston tried a variety of layouts and shades of colour. The scheme on this 1952 Leyland-bodied PD2 remained a one-off.** *Reg Wilson*
Opposite, bottom: **Preston undertook extensive rebuilds of eight of its all-Leyland PD2s, lengthening them to 30ft and converting them to forward entrance. The programme was spread over the period 1959-67.** *Geoff Lumb*

The 1968 North West Bus Handbook

RAMSBOTTOM

Ramsbottom Urban District Council, Stubbins Lane, Ramsbottom

In 1913 Ramsbottom UDC entered the transport business with three Railless trolleybuses on a service from Holcombe Brook to Edenfield. Motorbus operation started in 1922 with a solitary Thornycroft, and the trolleybus route was converted to motorbuses at the end of the decade, officially being abandoned in 1931.

The first Leylands - Lions - joined the fleet in 1927 and from that point on Leyland was Ramsbottom's sole supplier. Double-deck operation only started after World War II, with the delivery of six Titans in 1947. These were among the first examples of the new PD2 model to enter service, and Ramsbottom was also one of the first buyers of the underfloor-engined Royal Tiger, putting three into operation in 1950.

The future: Ramsbottom UDC Transport was absorbed by the SELNEC PTE in November 1969. Britain's last new half-cab double-decker, a PD3 Titan ordered by Ramsbottom, was delivered to SELNEC shortly after the takeover.

1	247STD	Leyland Titan PD2/24	East Lancashire	H35/28R	1961	
2	367XTE	Leyland Titan PD2/30	East Lancashire	H35/28R	1962	
3	9459TE	Leyland Titan PD2A/30	East Lancashire	H35/28F	1963	
4	LTD232C	Leyland Titan PD3A/1	East Lancashire	H41/32F	1965	
5	TTB879D	Leyland Titan PD3A/1	East Lancashire	H41/32F	1966	
6	DTC415E	Leyland Titan PD3/4	East Lancashire	H41/32F	1967	
7	DTC416E	Leyland Titan PD3/4	East Lancashire	H41/32F	1967	
8	FTF702F	Leyland Titan PD3/4	East Lancashire	H41/32F	1967	
9	FTF703F	Leyland Titan PD3/4	East Lancashire	H41/32F	1967	
12	RJX258	Albion Nimbus NS3AN	Weymann	B31F	1963	Warrington, Corporation 1967
17	HTB656	Leyland Tiger PS1	Roe	B35R	1946	
21	HTF816	Leyland Titan PD2/1	Leyland	H30/26R	1947	
29	MTC998	Leyland Titan PD2/3	Leyland	H30/26R	1951	

Livery: Maroon and cream

Ramsbottom, with just 13 buses, was the North West's smallest municipal fleet. All but one of its buses were Leylands, and the two oldest had Leyland bodies. Pictured outside the depot that was near Holcomb Brook is **29.** *Reg Wilson*

All of Ramsbottom's more modern Titans had East Lancs bodies, including number 1, a semi-automatic PD2/24. After moving on to Titans with St Helens fronts, Ramsbottom reverted to exposed radiators for its final Titans. *Roy Marshall*

RAWTENSTALL

Rawtenstall Corporation Motors, Bacup Road, Rawtenstall

Rawtenstall Corporation dabbled in early bus operation with two Ryknield double-deckers in 1908. They were withdrawn in 1910. In 1908 Rawtenstall took over and electrified the local tramway operations. Bus operation was tried again, with greater success, in 1924 with six Leyland single-deckers. Five Titans introduced double-deck bus operation in 1931 and hastened the demise of the trams - the last ran in March 1932. By the end of the decade there were almost 50 buses in the fleet and all were Leylands, all but two with Leyland bodywork. Indeed only one full-size non-Leyland bus was operated in the post-1930 Rawtenstall Corporation fleet, a solitary wartime Guy which, despite being non-standard, was rebodied in 1951 and survived until 1964.

The future: Rawtenstall and Haslingden merged on 1 April 1968 to form the Rossendale Joint Transport Committee. This was acquired by the newly-created Rossendale Borough Council in 1974 and became Rossendale Transport Ltd in 1986, remaining in local authority ownership and expanding its sphere of influence into Greater Manchester on tendered services.

1-10			Leyland Titan PD2/1		Leyland		H30/26R	1949		
1	KTE721	3	KTE723	5	KTE725	7	KTE727	9	KTE729
2	KTE722	4	KTE724	6	KTE726	8	KTE728	10	KTE730

16	NTD529	Leyland Titan PD2/1	Leyland	H30/26R	1951
17	RTC821	Leyland Titan PD2/12	Leyland	H31/25R	1953
18	RTC822	Leyland Titan PD2/12	Leyland	H31/25R	1953
19	RTC823	Leyland Titan PD2/12	Leyland	H31/25R	1953

Six PD2/20s delivered in 1955 were the only Rawtenstall buses with new-look fronts. These had East Lancs bodies and are represented by 27, which is seen in the bus station which is adjacent to the depot.
Roy Marshall

Rawtenstall bought two Leopards with neat East Lancs bodies in 1964. They were 44-seaters and were operated as driver-only buses from new. *Roy Marshall*

20	RTE534	Leyland Titan PD2/12	East Lancashire	H31/28R	1953		
21	RTE535	Leyland Titan PD2/12	East Lancashire	H31/28R	1953		
22	RTE536	Leyland Titan PD2/12	East Lancashire	H31/28R	1953		
23	RTE537	Leyland Titan PD2/12	East Lancashire	H31/28R	1953		

24-29		Leyland Titan PD2/20	East Lancashire	H31/28R	1955		
24	VTJ731	**26**	VTJ733	**27**	VTJ734	**28** VTJ735	**29** VTJ736
25	VTJ732						

30-41		Leyland Titan PD3/4	East Lancashire	H41/32F	1964-66		
30	FTE630B	**33** FTE633B	**36** MTJ436C	**38** XTJ938D	**40** XTJ940D		
31	FTE631B	**34** MTJ434C	**37** MTJ437C	**39** XTJ939D	**41** XTJ941D		
32	FTE632B	**35** MTJ435C					

	1386TF	Austin J2BA	Austin	M11	1963	
50	FTE650B	Leyland Leopard L1	East Lancashire	B44F	1964	
51	FTE651B	Leyland Leopard L1	East Lancashire	B44F	1964	
52	MTC255	Leyland Royal Tiger PSU1/13	Roe	B44F	1950	Ramsbottom, 1963
55	MTB848	Leyland Tiger PS2/1	East Lancashire	B35R	1950	
57	RTB49	Leyland Tiger Cub PSUC1/1	Weymann	B44F	1953	
58	466FTJ	Leyland Tiger Cub PSUC1/1	East Lancashire	B43F	1958	
59	738NTD	Leyland Tiger Cub PSUC1/1	East Lancashire	B43F	1958	

Vehicles ordered by Rawtenstall and delivered during 1968 to Rossendale Transport which was formed 1st April 1968.

52	JTF152F	Leyland Leopard PSU4/2R	East Lancashire	B44F	1968
53	JTF153F	Leyland Leopard PSU4/2R	East Lancashire	B44F	1968
54	JTF154F	Leyland Leopard PSU4/2R	East Lancashire	B44F	1968

Livery: Crimson and cream

RIBBLE

Ribble Motor Services Ltd, W C Standerwick Ltd, Scout Motor Services Ltd

Frenchwood Avenue, Preston, Lancashire

Ribble Motor Services was registered in 1919. In the following year the British Automobile Traction Co acquired a shareholding and in 1927 Ribble acquired sister BAT company Lancashire & Westmorland Motor Services. The limit of the company's northern expansion was Carlisle, and in 1931 it took over the Carlisle & District Transport Co.

The creation of the Tilling & British Automobile Traction Co in 1928 saw Ribble become a TBAT subsidiary and when that partnership was dissolved in 1942 ownership passed to the British Electric Traction group. By this time Ribble was a substantial operator covering an area from Carlisle down to the Mersey. It operated a network of local and interurban services throughout Lancashire.

The Standerwick coach operation was purchased in 1932. Other major acquisitions included Scout Motor Services of Preston (1961) and Bamber Bridge Motor Services (1967).

Ribble was a staunch supporter of its local chassis manufacture, buying the bulk of its buses and coaches from Leyland.

The future: Ribble became a subsidiary of the National Bus Company which took over the former BET group's bus operations on 1 January 1969. In readiness for NBC's privatisation the company's operating area was reduced in 1986 with its southern operations going to a new North Western company and its Carlisle-based fleet passing to Cumberland. The company was sold to its management in March 1988, at which time it was running 700 buses in Lancashire and Greater Manchester. It was subsequently purchased by Stagecoach in April 1989.

Standerwick coaches are 1-48 plus those with s suffix; Scout vehicles have S prefix.

1-7			Leyland Tiger Cub PSUC1/2T		Burlingham Seagull		C41F		1958	
1	NFR949	3		NFR951	5	NFR953	6	NFR954	7	NFR955
2	NFR950	4		NFR952						

16-37			Leyland Atlantean PDR1/1		Weymann		CH34/16FT 1960-61			
16	SFV412	21		SFV417	26	VFR368	30	VFR372	34	VFR376
17	SFV413	22		SFV418	27	VFR369	31	VFR373	35	VFR377
18	SFV414	23		SFV419	28	VFR370	32	VFR374	36	VFR378
19	SFV415	24		SFV420	29	VFR371	33	VFR375	37	VFR379
20	SFV416	25		SFV421						

Duple Donington coach bodies were relatively rare. In 1960 Scout bought four on Leyland Tiger Cub chassis. S54 is seen in Blackburn when running as part of the Ribble fleet with fleet number 1069. *Roy Marshall*

38-48

		Leyland Atlantean PDR1/1		Weymann		CH34/15FT 1959-60		

38	MCK812	41	NRN603	43	NRN605	45	NRN607	47	NRN609
39	NRN601	42	NRN604	44	NRN606	46	NRN608	48	NRN610
40	NRN602								

50s	FCK450G	Bristol VRL/LH6L	Eastern Coach Works	CH42/18CT	1968
S54	NRN166	Leyland Tiger Cub PSUC1/2	Duple Donington	C41F	1960
S55	NRN167	Leyland Tiger Cub PSUC1/2	Duple Donington	C41F	1960
S56	NRN168	Leyland Tiger Cub PSUC1/2	Duple Donington	C41F	1960
S57	NRN169	Leyland Tiger Cub PSUC1/2	Duple Donington	C41F	1960

58-62

		Leyland Leopard L2		Duple Donington		C41FT*	1961	*S62 is C34F

S58	PRN146	S59	PRN147	S60	PRN148	S61	PRN149	S62	PRN150

S63	TCK63	Leyland Leopard PSU3/3RT	Harrington Cavalier	C49F	1963
S64	TCK64	Leyland Leopard PSU3/3RT	Harrington Cavalier	C49F	1963
S65	TCK65	Leyland Leopard PSU3/3RT	Harrington Cavalier	C49F	1963
S66	NRN611	Leyland Atlantean PDR1/1	Weymann	CH34/16FT	1960
S67	NRN612	Leyland Atlantean PDR1/1	Weymann	CH34/16FT	1960
S68	NRN613	Leyland Atlantean PDR1/1	Weymann	CH34/16FT	1960
S69	NRN614	Leyland Atlantean PDR1/1	Weymann	CH34/16FT	1960

201-220

		Leyland Leopard PSU3/4R	Marshall	B45F	1967

201	ECK201E	205	ECK205E	209	ECK209E	213	ECK213E	217	ECK217E
202	ECK202E	206	ECK206E	210	ECK210E	214	ECK214E	218	ECK218E
203	ECK203E	207	ECK207E	211	ECK211E	215	ECK215E	219	ECK219E
204	ECK204E	208	ECK208E	212	ECK212E	216	ECK216E	220	ECK220E

221-230

				Brsitol RELL6L			Eastern Coach Works		B41D	1968

221	FRN221F	223	FRN223F	225	FRN225F	227	FRN227F	229	FRN229F
222	FRN222F	224	FRN224F	226	FRN226F	228	FRN228F	230	FRN230F

408-457

Leyland Tiger Cub PSUC1/1 — Saunders-Roe — B44F — 1953-54

408	ERN776	419	FCK851	429	FCK861	439	FCK871	448	FCK880
409	FCK841	420	FCK852	430	FCK862	440	FCK872	449	FCK881
410	FCK842	421	FCK853	431	FCK863	441	FCK873	450	FCK882
411	FCK843	422	FCK854	432	FCK864	442	FCK874	451	FCK883
412	FCK844	423	FCK855	433	FCK865	443	FCK875	453	FCK885
413	FCK845	424	FCK856	434	FCK866	444	FCK876	454	FCK886
415	FCK847	425	FCK857	435	FCK867	445	FCK877	455	FCK887
416	FCK848	426	FCK858	437	FCK869	446	FCK878	456	FCK888
417	FCK849	427	FCK859	438	FCK870	447	FCK879	457	FCK889
418	FCK850	428	FCK860						

458-497

Leyland Leopard PSU3/1R — Marshall — B53F — 1963

458	TCK458	466	TCK466	474	TCK474	482	TCK482	490	TCK490
459	TCK459	467	TCK467	475	TCK475	483	TCK483	491	TCK491
460	TCK460	468	TCK468	476	TCK476	484	TCK484	492	TCK492
461	TCK461	469	TCK469	477	TCK477	485	TCK485	493	TCK493
462	TCK462	470	TCK470	478	TCK478	486	TCK486	494	TCK494
463	TCK463	471	TCK471	479	TCK479	487	TCK487	495	TCK495
464	TCK464	472	TCK472	480	TCK480	488	TCK488	496	TCK496
465	TCK465	473	TCK473	481	TCK481	489	TCK489	497	TCK497

498-547

Leyland Leopard PSU3/1R — Marshall — B53F — 1964

498	UCK498	508	UCK508	518	UCK518	528	UCK528	538	UCK538
499	UCK499	509	UCK509	519	UCK519	529	UCK529	539	UCK539
500	UCK500	510	UCK510	520	UCK520	530	UCK530	540	UCK540
501	UCK501	511	UCK511	521	UCK521	531	UCK531	541	UCK541
502	UCK502	512	UCK512	522	UCK522	532	UCK532	542	UCK542
503	UCK503	513	UCK513	523	UCK523	533	UCK533	543	UCK543
504	UCK504	514	UCK514	524	UCK524	534	UCK534	544	UCK544
505	UCK505	515	UCK515	525	UCK525	535	UCK535	545	UCK545
506	UCK506	516	UCK516	526	UCK526	536	UCK536	546	UCK546
507	UCK507	517	UCK517	527	UCK527	537	UCK537	547	UCK547

548-567

Leyland Leopard PSU3/1R — Weymann — B53F* — 1964 — *many re-seated to B45F

548	ARN548B	552	ARN552B	556	ARN556B	560	ARN560B	564	ARN564B
549	ARN549B	553	ARN553B	557	ARN557B	561	ARN561B	565	ARN565B
550	ARN550B	554	ARN554B	558	ARN558B	562	ARN562B	566	ARN566B
551	ARN551B	555	ARN555B	559	ARN559B	563	ARN563B	567	ARN567B

568-587

Leyland Leopard PSU3/1R — Marshall — B53F* — 1965 — *many re-seated to B45F

568	ARN568C	572	ARN572C	576	ARN576C	580	ARN580C	584	ARN584C
569	ARN569C	573	ARN573C	577	ARN577C	581	ARN581C	585	ARN585C
570	ARN570C	574	ARN574C	578	ARN578C	582	ARN582C	586	ARN586C
571	ARN571C	575	ARN575C	579	ARN579C	583	ARN583C	587	ARN587C

588-607

Leyland Leopard PSU3/1R — Weymann — B53F* — 1965 — *many re-seated to B45F

588	ARN588C	592	ARN592C	596	ARN596C	600	ARN600C	604	ARN604C
589	ARN589C	593	ARN593C	597	ARN597C	601	ARN601C	605	ARN605C
590	ARN590C	594	ARN594C	598	ARN598C	602	ARN602C	606	ARN606C
591	ARN591C	595	ARN595C	599	ARN599C	603	ARN603C	607	ARN607C

Opposite, top: **Odd vehicles in the Ribble group of fleets were five Burlingham-bodied PD3/3s which had been new to Scout of Preston. These still carried Scout names, albeit on Ribble red livery, a feature introduced when the vehicles were placed into Ribble depots at Preston and Blackpool.** *Reg Wilson*
Opposite, bottom: **The 1967 double-deck arrivals were Northern Counties-bodied Leyland Atlanteans and were placed initially on service 55, the trunk route connecting Lancaster with Keswick. When new, the batch had examples with engine shrouds and standard indented rears. Pictured in Grasmere is 1963.** *Bill Potter*

608-627
Leyland Leopard PSU3/2R — Metro-Cammell — B53F — 1965

608	CCK608C	612	CCK612C	616	CCK616C	620	CCK620C	624	CCK624C
609	CCK609C	613	CCK613C	617	CCK617C	621	CCK621C	625	CCK625C
610	CCK610C	614	CCK614C	618	CCK618C	622	CCK622C	626	CCK626C
611	CCK611C	615	CCK615C	619	CCK619C	623	CCK623C	627	CCK627C

628-657
Leyland Leopard PSU4/2R — Marshall — B44F — 1966

628	CRN628D	634	CRN634D	640	CRN640D	646	CRN646D	652	CRN652D
629	CRN629D	635	CRN635D	641	CRN641D	647	CRN647D	653	CRN653D
630	CRN630D	636	CRN636D	642	CRN642D	648	CRN648D	654	CRN654D
631	CRN631D	637	CRN637D	643	CRN643D	649	CRN649D	655	CRN655D
632	CRN632D	638	CRN638D	644	CRN644D	650	CRN650D	656	CRN656D
633	CRN633D	639	CRN639D	645	CRN645D	651	CRN651D	657	CRN657D

658-682
Leyland Leopard PSU4/2R — Marshall — B44F — 1966

658	DRN658D	663	DRN663D	668	DRN668D	673	DRN673D	678	DRN678D
659	DRN659D	664	DRN664D	669	DRN669D	674	DRN674D	679	DRN679D
660	DRN660D	665	DRN665D	670	DRN670D	675	DRN675D	680	DRN680D
661	DRN661D	666	DRN666D	671	DRN671D	676	DRN676D	681	DRN681D
662	DRN662D	667	DRN667D	672	DRN672D	677	DRN677D	682	DRN682D

701-706
Leyland Leopard PSU3/3RT — Duple Continental — C40FT — 1962

701	SCK866	703	SCK869	704	SCK870	705	SCK871	706	SCK872
702	SCK867								

707-728
Leyland Leopard PSU3/3RT — Harrington Cavalier — C49F — 1963

707	TCK707	712	TCK712	717	TCK717	721	TCK721	725	TCK725
708	TCK708	713	TCK713	718	TCK718	722	TCK722	726	TCK726
709	TCK709	714	TCK714	719	TCK719	723	TCK723	727	TCK727
710	TCK710	715	TCK715	720	TCK720	724	TCK724	728	TCK728
711	TCK711	716	TCK716						

729s-763
Leyland Leopard PSU3/3RT — Plaxton Panorama — C49F — 1963-64

729s	TRN729	736s	TRN736	743	TRN743	750	TRN750	757	TRN757
730s	TRN730	737s	TRN737	744	TRN744	751	TRN751	758	TRN758
731s	TRN731	738s	TRN738	745	TRN745	752	TRN752	759	TRN759
732s	TRN732	S739	TRN739	746	TRN746	753	TRN753	760	TRN760
733s	TRN733	S740	TRN740	747	TRN747	754	TRN754	761	TRN761
734s	TRN734	S741	TRN741	748	TRN748	755	TRN755	762	TRN762
735s	TRN735	S742	TRN742	749	TRN749	756	TRN756	763	TRN763

Ribble took delivery of large numbers of Leyland Leopard buses to displace 53-seat double-decks, while still retaining conductors. In 1964 four with Marshall bodywork arrived at Fleetwood for local services and short workings on route 162. Pictured in Birch Street is 531.
Bill Potter

764-773 — Leyland Leopard PSU3/1RT — Marshall — DP49F — 1964

764	TRN764	766	TRN766	768	TRN768	770	TRN770	772	TRN772
765	TRN765	767	TRN767	769	TRN769	771	TRN771	773	TRN773

774	ACK774B	Leyland Panther PSUR1/2RT	Marshall	DP49F 1964

775-807 — Leyland Leopard PSU3/3RT — Plaxton Panorama — C49F — 1965

775	ARN775C	782	ARN782C	789	ARN789C	796s	ARN796C	802s	ARN802C
776	ARN776C	783	ARN783C	790	ARN790C	797s	ARN797C	803s	ARN803C
777	ARN777C	784	ARN784C	791	ARN791C	798s	ARN798C	S804	ARN804C
778	ARN778C	785	ARN785C	792	ARN792C	799s	ARN799C	S805	ARN805C
779	ARN779C	786	ARN786C	793	ARN793C	800s	ARN800C	S806	ARN806C
780	ARN780C	787	ARN787C	794	ARN794C	801s	ARN801C	S807	ARN807C
781	ARN781C	788	ARN788C	795s	ARN795C				

808-817 — Leyland Leopard PSU3/3RT — Weymann — DP49F — 1965

808	ARN808C	810	ARN810C	812	ARN812C	814	ARN814C	816	ARN816C
809	ARN809C	811	ARN811C	813	ARN813C	815	ARN815C	817	ARN817C

818-831 — Leyland Leopard PSU3/4R — Marshall — DP49F — 1966

818	CRN818D	821	CRN821D	824	CRN824D	827	CRN827D	830	CRN830D
819	CRN819D	822	CRN822D	825	CRN825D	828	CRN828D	831	CRN831D
820	CRN820D	823	CRN823D	826	CRN826D	829	CRN829D		

832-853 — Leyland Leopard PSU3/4R — Plaxton Panorama Elite — C49F* — 1966 — *842-853 are C44FT

832	CRN832D	837	CRN837D	842s	CRN842D	846s	CRN846D	S850	CRN850D
833	CRN833D	838	CRN838D	843s	CRN843D	847s	CRN847D	S851	CRN851D
834	CRN834D	839	CRN839D	844s	CRN844D	848s	CRN848D	S852	CRN852D
835	CRN835D	840	CRN840D	845s	CRN845D	849s	CRN849D	S853	CRN853D
836	CRN836D	841	CRN841D						

854-863 — Bedford VAM5 — Plaxton Panorama Elite — C32F — 1966

854	CRN854D	856	CRN856D	858	CRN858D	860	CRN860D	862	CRN862D
855	CRN855D	857	CRN857D	859	CRN859D	861	CRN861D	863	CRN863D

One of the biggest single orders for Plaxton's Panorama I body, as this style was known, called for 33 to be divided between Ribble, Standerwick and Scout. New in 1965, they were based on Leyland Leopard PSU3/3RT chassis with two-speed rear axles. To identify the fleets, Scout vehicles had an upper-case S prefix while Standerwick coaches had a lowercase s suffix. Shown here is 795s. *Reg Wilson*

864-889

Leyland Leopard PSU3/4R Plaxton Panorama Elite C49F* 1967 *888/9 are C44FT

864	ECK864E	870	ECK870E	875	ECK875E	880s	ECK880E	885s	ECK885E
865	ECK865E	871	ECK871E	876s	ECK876E	881s	ECK881E	S886	ECK886E
866	ECK866E	872	ECK872E	877s	ECK877E	882s	ECK882E	S887	ECK887E
867	ECK867E	873	ECK873E	878s	ECK878E	883s	ECK883E	S888	ECK888E
868	ECK868E	874	ECK874E	879s	ECK879E	884s	ECK884E	S889	ECK889E
869	ECK869E								

890-903

Leyland Leopard PSU3/4R Marshall DP49F 1967

890	ECK890E	893	ECK893E	896	ECK896E	899	ECK899E	902	ECK902E
891	ECK891E	894	ECK894E	897	ECK897E	900	ECK900E	903	ECK903E
892	ECK892E	895	ECK895E	898	ECK898E	901	ECK901E		

904-933

Leyland Leopard PSU3/4R Willowbrook DP49F 1968

904	FCK904F	910	FCK910F	916	FCK916F	922	FCK922F	928	FCK928F
905	FCK905F	911	FCK911F	917	FCK917F	923	FCK923F	929	FCK929F
906	FCK906F	912	FCK912F	918	FCK918F	924	FCK924F	930	FCK930F
907	FCK907F	913	FCK913F	919	FCK919F	925	FCK925F	931	FCK931F
908	FCK908F	914	FCK914F	920	FCK920F	926	FCK926F	932	FCK932F
909	FCK909F	915	FCK915F	921	FCK921F	927	FCK927F	933	FCK933F

934-945

Leyland Leopard PSU3/4R Plaxton Panorama Elite C49F 1968

934s	FCK934F	937s	FCK937F	940s	FCK940F	S942	FCK942F	S944	FCK944F
935s	FCK935F	938s	FCK938F	941s	FCK941F	S943	FCK943F	S945	FCK945F
936s	FCK936F	939s	FCK939F						

989-1018

Leyland Tiger Cub PSUC1/2 Burlingham Seagull C41F 1958

989	LCK703	995	LCK709	1001	LCK715	1008	LCK722	1014	LCK728
990	LCK704	996	LCK710	1002	LCK716	1009	LCK723	1015	LCK729
992	LCK706	997	LCK711	1004	LCK718	1010	LCK724	1016	LCK730
993	LCK707	998	LCK712	1006	LCK720	1012	LCK726	1017	LCK731
994	LCK708	1000	LCK714	1007	LCK721	1013	LCK727	1018	LCK732

1019-1053

Leyland Leopard L2T Harrington Cavalier C41F* 1961 *1029-48 are C32F

1019	PCK601	1026	PCK608	1033	PCK615	1040	PCK622	1047	PCK629
1020	PCK602	1027	PCK609	1034	PCK616	1041	PCK623	1048	PCK630
1021	PCK603	1028	PCK610	1035	PCK617	1042	PCK624	1049	PCK631
1022	PCK604	1029	PCK611	1036	PCK618	1043	PCK625	1050	PCK632
1023	PCK605	1030	PCK612	1037	PCK619	1044	PCK626	1051	PCK633
1024	PCK606	1031	PCK613	1038	PCK620	1045	PCK627	1052	PCK634
1025	PCK607	1032	PCK614	1039	PCK621	1046	PCK628	1053	PCK635

1060	821YEH	Leyland Leopard L2T	Plaxton Panorama Elite	C41F	1963	Michelin Tyres, 1963
1061	822YEH	Leyland Leopard L2T	Plaxton Panorama Elite	C41F	1963	Michelin Tyres, 1963

1062-1068

Leyland Tiger Cub PSUC1/2 Burlingham Seagull C41F 1958

1062	NFR956	1064	NFR958	1066	NFR960	1067	NFR961	1068	NFR962
1063	NFR957	1065	NFR959						

1266-1285

Leyland Atlantean PDR1/1 Weymann CH39/20F 1962

1266	RRN415	1270	RRN419	1274	RRN423	1278	RRN427	1252	RRN431
1267	RRN416	1271	RRN420	1275	RRN424	1279	RRN428	1253	RRN432
1268	RRN417	1272	RRN421	1276	RRN425	1280	RRN429	1254	RRN433
1269	RRN418	1273	RRN422	1277	RRN426	1281	RRN430	1255	RRN434

Opposite, top: **Ribble provided coaches for express services as well as its own extensive tour programme. The mainstay of the tour coaches were 30ft Harrington Cavaliers, though in 1966 ten Bedfords joined the company and were based at Bury. Harrington coaches were also used on the company's Scottish services. Seen outside Fleetwood depot is 720.** *Bill Potter*
Opposite, bottom: **Ribble used Michelin Tyres and in 1963 purchased two coaches that had been used for tyre development by Michelin. These were numbered 1060 and 1061, the latter shown here while on an excursion in south Lakeland.** *Bill Potter*

1381-1405 Leyland Titan PD2/13 Metro-Cammell H33/28RD 1955

1381	HCK461	1386	HRN26	1391	HRN31	S1396	HRN36	1401	HRN41
1382	HCK463	1387	HRN27	1392	HRN32	1397	HRN37	1402	HRN42
1383	HCK464	1388	HRN28	1393	HRN33	1398	HRN38	1403	HRN43
1384	HCK465	1389	HRN29	1394	HRN34	1399	HRN39	1404	HRN44
1385	HCK466	1390	HRN30	1395	HRN35	1400	HRN40	1405	HRN45

1406-1430 Leyland Titan PD2/13 Metro-Cammell H33/28R 1955

1406	HCK462	1411	HCK471	1416	HCK476	1421	HCK481	1426	HRN21
1407w	HCK467	1412	HCK472	1417	HCK477	1422	HCK482	1427	HRN22
1408	HCK468	1413	HCK473	1418	HCK478	1423	HCK483	1428	HRN23
1409	HCK469	1414	HCK474	1419	HCK479	1424	HCK484	1429	HRN24
1410	HCK470	1415	HCK475	1420	HCK480	1425	HCK485	1430	HRN25

1431-1470 Leyland Titan PD2/12 Burlingham H33/28RD 1956

1431	JCK506	1439	JCK514	S1447	JCK522	1455	JCK530	1463	JCK538
1432	JCK507	1440	JCK515	1448	JCK523	S1456	JCK531	1464	JCK539
1433	JCK508	1441	JCK516	1449	JCK524	1457	JCK532	1465	JCK540
1434	JCK509	1442	JCK517	1450	JCK525	1458	JCK533	1466	JCK541
1435	JCK510	1443	JCK518	1451	JCK526	1459	JCK534	1467	JCK542
1436	JCK511	1444	JCK519	1452	JCK527	1460	JCK535	1468	JCK543
1437	JCK512	1445	JCK520	1453	JCK528	1461	JCK536	1469	JCK544
1438	JCK513	S1446	JCK521	1454	JCK529	1462	JCK537	1470	JCK545

1471-1475 Leyland Titan PD2/13 Burlingham H33/28R 1956

1471	JCK546	1472	JCK547	1473	JCK548	1474	JCK549	1475	JCK550

1476-1500 Leyland Titan PD2/12 Metro-Cammell H33/28R 1956

1476	JRN43	1481	JRN48	1486	JRN53	1491	JRN58	1496	JRN63
1477	JRN44	1482	JRN49	1487	JRN54	1492	JRN59	1497	JRN64
1478	JRN45	1483	JRN50	1488	JRN55	1493	JRN60	1498	JRN65
1479	JRN46	1484	JRN51	1489	JRN56	1494	JRN61	1499	JRN66
1480	JRN47	1485	JRN52	1490	JRN57	1495	JRN62	1500	JRN67

1501-1605 Leyland Titan PD3/4 Burlingham FH41/31F 1957-58

1501	KCK847	1522	KCK868	1543	KCK904	1564	KCK925	1585	LCK748
1502	KCK848	1523	KCK869	1544	KCK905	1565	KCK926	1586	LCK749
1503	KCK849	1524	KCK870	1545	KCK906	1566	KCK927	1587	LCK750
1504	KCK850	1525	KCK871	1546	KCK907	1567	KCK928	1588	LCK751
1505	KCK851	1526	KCK872	1547	KCK908	1568	KCK929	1589	LCK752
1506	KCK852	1527	KCK873	1548	KCK909	1569	KCK930	1590	LCK753
1507	KCK853	1528	KCK874	1549	KCK910	1570	LCK733	1591	LCK754
1508	KCK854	1529	KCK875	1550	KCK911	1571	LCK734	1592	LCK755
1509	KCK855	1530	KCK876	1551	KCK912	1572	LCK735	1593	LCK756
1510	KCK856	1531	KCK877	1552	KCK913	1573	LCK736	1594	LCK757
1511	KCK857	1532	KCK878	1553	KCK914	1574	LCK737	1595	LCK758
1512	KCK858	1533	KCK879	1554	KCK915	1575	LCK738	1596	LCK759
1513	KCK859	1534	KCK880	1555	KCK916	1576	LCK739	1597	LCK760
1514	KCK860	1535	KCK881	1556	KCK917	1577	LCK740	1598	LCK761
1515	KCK861	1536	KCK882	1557	KCK918	1578	LCK741	1599	LCK762
1516	KCK862	1537	KCK883	1558	KCK919	1579	LCK742	1600	LCK763
1517	KCK863	1538	KCK884	1559	KCK920	1580	LCK743	1601	LCK764
1518	KCK864	1539	KCK885	1560	KCK921	1581	LCK744	1602	LCK765
1519	KCK865	1540	KCK886	1561	KCK922	1582	LCK745	1603	LCK766
1520	KCK866	1541	KCK887	1562	KCK923	1583	LCK746	1604	LCK767
1521	KCK867	1542	KCK903	1563	KCK924	1584	LCK747	1605	LCK768

Ribble was one of the biggest subsidiaries of the BET group and its fleet was made up primarily of Leylands. While Leopards took over from 53-seat double-decks the 61-seaters continued on the busier routes. One of 20 Metro-Cammel-bodied Leyland Titans from 1956, 1490, is seen waiting time for the Knott End ferry. *Bill Potter*

After purchasing several batches of Atlantean, Ribble reverted to the Titan for batches in 1961 and 1962, both with MCW bodies. From the first batch is 1781. *Bill Potter*

A year after the last of the Lowlanders arrived, Ribble had found an altogether more attractive solution to its need for lowheight buses, and ordered ten PDR1/2 Atlanteans with Alexander bodies. The batch remained unique in the Ribble fleet. In 1968 these were based at Blackburn (5), Chorley (2), Fleetwood, Preston, and Clitheroe, whose 1870, is seen in Manchester. *Roy Marshall*

1606-1655 Leyland Atlantean PDR1/1 Metro-Cammell H44/34F 1959-60

1606	NCK347	1616	NCK357	1626	NCK367	1636	NCK625	1646	NCK635
1607	NCK348	1617	NCK358	1627	NCK368	1637	NCK626	1647	NCK636
1608	NCK349	1618	NCK359	1628	NCK369	1638	NCK627	1648	NCK637
1609	NCK350	1619	NCK360	1629	NCK370	1639	NCK628	1649	NCK638
1610	NCK351	1620	NCK361	1630	NCK371	1640	NCK629	1650	NCK639
1611	NCK352	1621	NCK362	1631	NCK372	1641	NCK630	1651	NCK640
1612	NCK353	1622	NCK363	1632	NCK621	1642	NCK631	1652	NCK641
1613	NCK354	1623	NCK364	1633	NCK622	1643	NCK632	1653	NCK642
1614	NCK355	1624	NCK365	1634	NCK623	1644	NCK633	1654	NCK643
1615	NCK356	1625	NCK366	1635	NCK624	1645	NCK634	1655	NCK644

1656-1680 Leyland Atlantean PDR1/1 Metro-Cammell L39/33F 1960

1656	NRN556	1661	NRN561	1666	NRN566	1671	NRN571	1676	NRN576
1657	NRN557	1662	NRN562	1667	NRN567	1672	NRN572	1677	NRN577
1658	NRN558	1663	NRN563	1668	NRN568	1673	NRN573	1678	NRN578
1659	NRN559	1664	NRN564	1669	NRN569	1674	NRN574	1679	NRN579
1660	NRN560	1665	NRN565	1670	NRN570	1675	NRN575	1680	NRN580

1681-1700 Leyland Atlantean PDR1/1 Metro-Cammell H44/34F 1960

1681	NRN581	1685	NRN585	1689	NRN589	1693	NRN593	1697	NRN597
1682	NRN582	1686	NRN586	1690	NRN590	1694	NRN594	1698	NRN598
1683	NRN583	1687	NRN587	1691	NRN591	1695	NRN595	1699	NRN599
1684	NRN584	1688	NRN588	1692	NRN592	1696	NRN596	1700	NRN600

1701-1705 Leyland Atlantean PDR1/1 Metro-Cammell L39/33F 1961

1701	PCK334	1702	PCK335	1703	PCK336	1704	PCK337	1705	PCK338

Ribble bought Atlanteans with both full-height and lowbridge bodywork. On the latter the upper deck had conventional seating at the front, but a side gangway and raised bench seating at the rear. Two are seen in Wigan, with the leading vehicle, 1677, NRN577, carrying an appropriate destination. *Stewart J Brown*

1706-1755   Leyland Titan PD3/5   Metro-Cammell   FH41/31F   1961

1706	PCK347	1716	PCK357	1726	PCK367	1736	PCK377	1746	PCK387
1707	PCK348	1717	PCK358	1727	PCK368	1737	PCK378	1747	PCK388
1708	PCK349	1718	PCK359	1728	PCK369	1738	PCK379	1748	PCK389
1709	PCK350	1719	PCK360	1729	PCK370	1739	PCK380	1749	PCK390
1710	PCK351	1720	PCK361	1730	PCK371	1740	PCK381	1750	PCK391
1711	PCK352	1721	PCK362	1731	PCK372	1741	PCK382	1751	PCK392
1712	PCK353	1722	PCK363	1732	PCK373	1742	PCK383	1752	PCK393
1713	PCK354	1723	PCK364	1733	PCK374	1743	PCK384	1753	PCK394
1714	PCK355	1724	PCK365	1734	PCK375	1744	PCK385	1754	PCK395
1715	PCK356	1725	PCK366	1735	PCK376	1745	PCK386	1755	PCK396

1756-1800   Leyland Titan PD3/5   Metro-Cammell   FH41/31F   1962

1756	RCK901	1765	RCK910	1774	RCK919	1783	RCK928	1792	RCK937
1757	RCK902	1766	RCK911	1775	RCK920	1784	RCK929	1793	RCK938
1758	RCK903	1767	RCK912	1776	RCK921	1785	RCK930	1794	RCK939
1759	RCK904	1768	RCK913	1777	RCK922	1786	RCK931	1795	RCK940
1760	RCK905	1769	RCK914	1778	RCK923	1787	RCK932	1796	RCK941
1761	RCK906	1770	RCK915	1779	RCK924	1788	RCK933	1797	RCK942
1762	RCK907	1771	RCK916	1780	RCK925	1789	RCK934	1798	RCK943
1763	RCK908	1772	RCK917	1781	RCK926	1790	RCK935	1799	RCK944
1764	RCK909	1773	RCK918	1782	RCK927	1791	RCK936	1800	RCK945

1801-1814   Leyland Atlantean PDR1/1   Metro-Cammell   L39/33F   1962

1801	RRN401	1804	RRN404	1807	RRN407	1810	RRN410	1813	RRN413
1802	RRN402	1805	RRN405	1808	RRN408	1811	RRN411	1814	RRN414
1803	RRN403	1806	RRN406	1809	RRN409	1812	RRN412		

1815-1850 — Leyland Titan PD3/5 — Metro-Cammell — H41/31F — 1963

1815	TCK815	1823	TCK823	1830	TCK830	1837	TCK837	1844	TCK844
1816	TCK816	1824	TCK824	1831	TCK831	1838	TCK838	1845	TCK845
1817	TCK817	1825	TCK825	1832	TCK832	1839	TCK839	1846	TCK846
1818	TCK818	1826	TCK826	1833	TCK833	1840	TCK840	1847	TCK847
1819	TCK819	1827	TCK827	1834	TCK834	1841	TCK841	1848	TCK848
1820	TCK820	1828	TCK828	1835	TCK835	1842	TCK842	1849	TCK849
1821	TCK821	1829	TCK829	1836	TCK836	1843	TCK843	1850	TCK850
1822	TCK822								

1851-1866 — Albion Lowlander LR1 — Alexander C — H41/31F — 1964-65

1851	UCK851	1855	UCK855	1858	UCK858	1861	ARN861C	1864	ARN864C
1852	UCK852	1856	UCK856	1859	UCK859	1862	ARN862C	1865	ARN865C
1853	UCK853	1857	UCK857	1860	UCK860	1863	ARN863C	1866	ARN866C
1854	UCK854								

1867-1876 — Leyland Atlantean PDR1/2 — Alexander H — H41/31F — 1966

1867	CRN867D	1869	CRN869D	1871	CRN871D	1873	CRN873D	1875	CRN875D
1868	CRN868D	1870	CRN870D	1872	CRN872D	1874	CRN874D	1876	CRN876D

1951-1965 — Leyland Atlantean PDR1/2 — Northern Counties — H41/31F — 1967

1951	ECK951E	1954	ECK954E	1957	ECK957E	1960	ECK960E	1963	ECK963E
1952	ECK952E	1955	ECK955E	1958	ECK958E	1961	ECK961E	1964	ECK964E
1953	ECK953E	1956	ECK956E	1959	ECK959E	1962	ECK962E	1965	ECK965E

1966	661KTJ	Leyland Atlantean PDR1/1	Weymann	L39/34F	1959	Bamber Bridge Motor Services, 1967
1967	2295TE	Leyland Atlantean PDR1/1	Weymann	L39/33F	1963	Bamber Bridge Motor Services, 1967
1968	747EUS	Albion Lowlander LR1	Alexander C	H41/31F	1962	Bamber Bridge Motor Services, 1967
S1	OCK500	Leyland Atlantean PDR1/1	Metro-Cammell	H44/34F	1960	
S2	398JTB	Leyland Atlantean PDR1/1	Metro-Cammell	H44/33F	1959	Leyland demonstrator, 1960
S3	PRN143	Leyland Atlantean PDR1/1	Metro-Cammell	H44/33F	1961	
S4	PRN144	Leyland Atlantean PDR1/1	Metro-Cammell	H44/33F	1961	
S5	PRN145	Leyland Atlantean PDR1/1	Metro-Cammell	H44/33F	1961	

S21-25 — Leyland Titan PD3/3 — Burlingham — H41/31F — 1958-59

S21	LRN62	S22	LRN63	S23	MCK369	S24	MCK370	S25	MCK371

Livery: 'Ribble Red' and cream.

Note: Scout Motor Services, while had used Ribble red livery for several years, was fully absorbed by Ribble in October 1968. S1-5/21-25 were renumbered 1969-78 while the others lost their S prefix.

After buying lowbridge Atlanteans, Ribble switched to the lowheight Albion Lowlander. It specified Alexander bodywork but with the addition of a full-width cab to match its large fleet of PD3 Titans. One from the second batch, 1864, waits in Bolton bus station, ready to leave for Chorley.
Roy Marshall

ROCHDALE

Rochdale Corporation Transport, Mellor Street, Rochdale

Municipal trams took over from previous company operations in Rochdale in 1902. The system operated until 1932. Motorbuses were introduced in 1926. By 1932 the fleet numbered almost 100 and included some of the country's first diesel-engined buses, double-deck Crossley Condors.

The first AECs, two Regents, entered service in 1935. AEC would be Rochdale's main supplier of buses after World War II. Leyland supplied a small number of Titans and Tigers between 1936 and 1940, in sharp contrast to its domination of many north-west municipal fleets. The last Leyland to join Rochdale's operation was a Titan acquired from Yelloway Motor Services in 1944 consequent upon Yelloway giving up its service to Manchester.

Daimler was a secondary supplier of Rochdale's buses from 1938 but in the absence of a rear-engined double-deck model from AEC it was to the Fleetline that Rochdale turned in 1964 for its double-deck requirements.

The future: Rochdale Corporation Transport was absorbed by the SELNEC PTE in November 1969.

4	HDK704	AEC Regal IV 9821E	East Lancashire	B44F	1951	
7	HDK707	AEC Regal IV 9821E	East Lancashire	B44F	1951	
8	JDK708	AEC Regal IV 9822E	Burlingham	B44F	1953	
9	JDK709	AEC Regal IV 9822E	Burlingham	B44F	1953	
12	JDK712	AEC Regal IV 9822E	Burlingham	B44F	1953	

16-20		AEC Reliance 2MU3RA	Weymann	B42D	1961	
16 2116DK	**17** 2117DK	**18** 2118DK	**19** 2119DK	**20** 2120DK		

21	6321DK	AEC Reliance 2MU3RA	East Lancashire	B42D	1964
22	ADK722B	AEC Reliance 2MU2RA	East Lancashire	B43D	1964
23	ADK723B	AEC Reliance 2MU2RA	East Lancashire	B43D	1964

Having won Rochdale's business from Daimler, AEC lost out when it came to high-capacity double-deckers as Rochdale started ordering small batches of Fleetlines. The first five, in 1964, had Metro-Cammell bodywork represented by 323. *Roy Marshall*

In 1953-54 Rochdale took its last half-cab Daimlers. These were CVG6s with Weymann bodywork. Subsequent orders went to AEC. *Roy Marshall*

24-29

		AEC Reliance 6MU2RA		Willowbrook		B45F	1966		
24	GDK324D	25	GDK325D	26	GDK326D	27	GDK327D	28	GDK328D

30	LDK730G	Daimler Fleetline SRG6LX	Willowbrook		B45F	1968	
31	LDK731G	Daimler Fleetline SRG6LX	Willowbrook		B45F	1968	
32	LDK732G	Daimler Fleetline SRG6LX	Willowbrook		B45F	1968	
33	LDK733G	Daimler Fleetline SRG6LX	Willowbrook		B45F	1968	

223-232

		AEC Regent III 9612E		Weymann		H31/28R	1949-50		
221	GDK721	225	HDK25	227	HDK27	229	HDK29	231	HDK31
223	HDK23	226	HDK26	228	HDK28	230	HDK30	232	HDK32
224	HDK24								

233-237

		AEC Regent III 9612E		East Lancashire		H31/28R	1952		
233	HDK833	234	HDK834	235	HDK835	236	HDK836	237	HDK837

238-267

		Daimler CVG6		Weymann		H31/28R	1953-54		
238	JDK738	244	JDK744	250	JDK750	256	KDK656	262	KDK662
239	JDK739	245	JDK745	251	JDK751	257	KDK657	263	KDK663
240	JDK740	246	JDK746	252	JDK752	258	KDK658	264	KDK664
241	JDK741	247	JDK747	253	KDK653	259	KDK659	265	KDK665
242	JDK742	248	JDK748	254	KDK654	260	KDK660	266	KDK666
243	JDK743	249	JDK749	255	KDK655	261	KDK661	267	KDK667

Rochdale Corporation was one of the few buyers of AEC Regent Vs with Gardner engines. Forty were delivered in 1956 and from that batch 301, is seen leaving the town for Norden. They had 61-seat Weymann bodies. *Reg Wilson*

268-307

AEC Regent V 6LW D2RA6G Weymann H33/28R 1956

268	NDK968	276	NDK976	284	NDK984	292	NDK992	300	ODK700
269	NDK969	277	NDK977	285	NDK985	293	NDK993	301	ODK701
270	NDK970	278	NDK978	286	NDK986	294	NDK994	302	ODK702
271	NDK971	279	NDK979	287	NDK987	295	NDK995	303	ODK703
272	NDK972	280	NDK980	288	NDK988	296	NDK996	304	ODK704
273	NDK973	281	NDK981	289	NDK989	297	NDK997	305	ODK705
274	NDK974	282	NDK982	290	NDK990	298	ODK698	306	ODK706
275	NDK975	283	NDK983	291	NDK991	299	ODK699	307	ODK707

308-318

AEC Regent V D2RA Weymann H33/28R 1957

308	RDK408	311	RDK411	313	RDK413	315	RDK415	317	RDK417
309	RDK409	312	RDK412	314	RDK414	316	RDK416	318	RDK418
310	RDK410								

319	TDK319	AEC Regent V D2RA	Weymann	H33/28RD	1959
320	TDK319	AEC Regent V D2RA	Weymann	H33/28RD	1959
321	TDK319	AEC Regent V D2RA	Weymann	H33/28RD	1959
322	TDK319	AEC Regent V D2RA	Weymann	H33/28RD	1959

323-334

Daimler Fleetline CRG6LX Weymann H43/34F 1964-65

323	6323DK	326	6326DK	329	EDK129C	331	EDK131C	333	EDK133C
324	6324DK	327	6327DK	330	EDK130C	332	EDK132C	334	EDK134C
325	6325DK	328	EDK128C						

335-344

Daimler Fleetline CRG6LX Metro-Cammell H43/34F 1968

335	KDK135F	337	KDK137F	339	KDK139F	341	KDK141F	343	KDK143F
336	KDK136F	338	KDK138F	340	KDK140F	342	KDK142F	344	KDK144F

Livery: Cream and navy

ST HELENS

St Helens Corporation Transport, Shaw Street, St Helens

St Helens was a comparative late-comer to municipal tramway operation, taking over the operations of the New St Helens and District Tramways Company and its 36 electric tramcars in 1919. Motorbus operation started in 1923 and trolleybuses followed in 1927. When the tramway system closed in 1936 St Helens was running 36 trolleybuses and 28 motorbuses.

The Corporation continued buying trolleybuses until 1951, but from 1952 started replacing time-expired trolleybuses with new motorbuses. Trolleybus operation ceased in 1958. The fleet was generally made up mainly of Leylands and AECs, the latter including some London-style RT-type Regent IIIs. All pre-1950 double-deckers (including trolleybuses) were of lowbridge design.

St Helens buses could be seen far beyond the town's boundaries on jointly-operated services which took them to places as far apart as Liverpool and Wigan.

The future: St Helens was absorbed by the expanded Merseyside PTE in 1974.

L1-L7 — AEC Regent V 2D3RV — Metro-Cammell — H36/28R — 1961

1	ODJ941	3	ODJ943	5	ODJ945	6	ODJ946	7	ODJ947
2	ODJ942	4	ODJ944						

L8-L12 — Leyland Titan PD2A/30 — East Lancashire — H36/28R — 1961

8	PDJ708	9	PDJ709	10	PDJ710	11	PDJ711	12	PDJ712

L13-L25 — Leyland Titan PD2A/30 — Metro-Cammell — H36/28R — 1962

13	PDJ813	16	PDJ816	19	PDJ819	22	RDJ102	24	RDJ104
14	PDJ814	17	PDJ817	20	RDJ100	23	RDJ103	25	RDJ105
15	PDJ815	18	PDJ818	21	RDJ101				

L26-L32 — Leyland Titan PD2A/30 — East Lancashire — H36/28R — 1962

26	RDJ726	28	RDJ728	30	RDJ730	31	RDJ731	32	RDJ732
27	RDJ727	29	RDJ729						

L33-L40 — AEC Regent V 2D3RV — Metro-Cammell — H36/28R — 1962

33	SDJ353	35	SDJ355	37	SDJ357	39	SDJ359	40	SDJ360
34	SDJ354	36	SDJ356	38	SDJ358				

L41-L45 — Leyland Titan PD2A/30 — East Lancashire — H36/28R — 1965

41	FDJ341C	42	FDJ342C	43	FDJ343C	44	FDJ344C	45	FDJ345C

46	FDJ346C	Leyland Titan PD2A/30	Metro-Cammell	H36/28R	1965
47	FDJ347C	Leyland Titan PD2A/30	Metro-Cammell	H36/28R	1965
48	FDJ348C	Leyland Titan PD2A/30	Metro-Cammell	H36/28R	1966
49	FDJ349C	Leyland Titan PD2A/30	Metro-Cammell	H36/28R	1966

St Helens Corporation gave its name to the revised new-look front adopted by Leyland in 1960 which was signified by an A suffix to the PD2 and PD3 chassis designation. The first of the line, K172, a PD2A/30, hid the conservative combination of synchromesh gearbox and vacuum brakes behind its new fibre-glass front. Weymann built the body. *Roy Marshall*

50-55

						Leyland Titan PD2A/27	East Lancashire	H37/28R	1967		

50	MDJ550E	52	MDJ552E	53	MDJ553E	54	MDJ554E	55	MDJ555E
51	MDJ551E								

56	MDJ916E	AEC Regent V 2D3RA	Metro-Cammell	H37/28R	1967
57	MDJ917E	AEC Regent V 2D3RA	Metro-Cammell	H37/28R	1967
58	MDJ918E	AEC Regent V 2D3RA	Metro-Cammell	H37/28R	1967
E84	DDJ491	Leyland Titan PD2/22	East Lancashire	H30/28R	1954
E87	DDJ525	Leyland Titan PD2/22	East Lancashire	H30/28R	1954
E88	DDJ526	Leyland Titan PD2/22	East Lancashire	H30/28R	1954
E90	DDJ528	Leyland Titan PD2/22	East Lancashire	H30/28R	1954

F101-F109

						Leyland Titan PD2/20	East Lancashire	H33/28R	1955		

101	EDJ501	103	EDJ503	105	EDJ505	107	EDJ507	109	EDJ509
102	EDJ502	104	EDJ504	106	EDJ506	108	EDJ508		

F112	EDJ512	Leyland Titan PD2/20	Davies/Park Royal	H33/28R	1956

F113-F117

					Leyland Titan PD2/20	Weymann	H33/28R	1956-57	

113	EDJ513	114	EDJ514	115	EDJ515	116	EDJ516	117	EDJ517

G118-G127

						Leyland Titan PD2/20	East Lancashire	H33/28R	1956-57		

118	FDJ818	122	FDJ822	124	FDJ824	126	FDJ826	127	FDJ827
121	FDJ821	123	FDJ823						

G128-G133

		Leyland Titan PD2/20		Weymann		H33/28R	1956		
128	FDJ828	130	FDJ830	131	FDJ831	132	FDJ832	133	FDJ833
129	FDJ829								

H134-H139

		AEC Regent V MD3RV		Weymann		H33/28R	1957		
134	GDJ434	136	GDJ436	137	GDJ437	138	GDJ438	139	GDJ439
135	GDJ435								

J140-J155

		AEC Regent V D3RV		Weymann		H33/28R	1958		
140	HDJ740	144	HDJ744	147	HDJ747	150	HDJ750	153	HDJ753
141	HDJ741	145	HDJ745	148	HDJ748	151	HDJ751	154	HDJ754
142	HDJ742	146	HDJ746	149	HDJ749	152	HDJ752	155	HDJ755
143	HDJ743								

J156-J163

		AEC Regent V D3RV		East Lancashire		H33/28R	1958		
156	HDJ756	158	HDJ758	160	HDJ760	162	HDJ762	163	HDJ763
157	HDJ757	159	HDJ759	161	HDJ761				

K164-K171

		AEC Regent V MD3RV		Weymann		H33/28R	1959		
164	KDJ364	166	KDJ366	168	KDJ368	170	KDJ370	171	KDJ371
165	KDJ365	167	KDJ367	169	KDJ369				

K172	LDJ982	Leyland Titan PD2/30	Weymann	H36/28R	1960
K173	LDJ983	Leyland Titan PD2/30	Weymann	H36/28R	1960
K174	LDJ984	Leyland Titan PD2/30	Weymann	H36/28R	1960
K175	LDJ985	Leyland Titan PD2/30	Weymann	H36/28R	1960
K176	LDJ986	Leyland Titan PD2/30	East Lancashire	H36/28R	1960
K177	LDJ987	Leyland Titan PD2/30	East Lancashire	H36/28R	1960
K178	LDJ988	Leyland Titan PD2/30	East Lancashire	H36/28R	1960
K179	LDJ989	Leyland Titan PD2/30	East Lancashire	H36/28R	1960
K199	KDJ999	AEC Regent V 2D3RA	East Lancashire	H41/32F	1959
200	SDJ162	Leyland Leopard L2	Duple Britannia	C41C	1962

210-214

		AEC Reliance 2MU3RA		Marshall		B45F*	1963-65	*213-4 are B41D	
210	TDJ610	211	TDJ611	212	TDJ612	213	DDJ213C	214	DDJ214C

215-232

		AEC Swift MP2R		Marshall		B44D	1968		
215	RDJ215F	219	RDJ219F	223	RDJ223F	227	TDJ227G	230	TDJ230G
216	RDJ216F	220	RDJ220F	224	TDJ224G	228	TDJ228G	231	TDJ231G
217	RDJ217F	221	RDJ221F	225	TDJ225G	229	TDJ229G	232	TDJ232G
218	RDJ218F	222	RDJ222F	226	TDJ226G				

On order: 9 AEC Swift/Marshall
Livery: Red and cream

Opposite, top: **St Helens never owned any rear-engined double-deckers, moving from half-cab Regents and Titans in 1967 to dual-door one-man-operated AEC Swifts in 1968. Marshall supplied the bodywork, adding St Helens to a small but growing band of new municipal customers for the Cambridge-based coachbuilder.** *Reg Wilson*
Opposite, bottom: **Orders at St Helens were shared between Leyland and AEC and the fleet's 1962 intake consisted of both types. AEC supplied eight Regent Vs with Metro-Cammell Orion bodies.** *Reg Wilson*

SALFORD

Salford City Transport, Frederick Road, Salford

In 1901 Salford Corporation took over and electrified those services in its area operated by the Manchester Carriage and Tramways Co. Bus operation started in 1920 with seven new Leylands, and expanded through the decade, with joint working with other operators. The tramway system was progressively replaced by buses during the 1930s, most of which were supplied by AEC and Leyland.

In 1950-52 there was a massive fleet renewal programme which saw 210 Daimlers replace virtually the entire pre-war fleet to give Salford one of the most modern bus fleets in Britain. After that no new buses were purchased for 10 years, with double-deck orders initially being placed with Daimler and Leyland and then entirely with the latter manufacturer.

The future: Salford City Transport was absorbed by the SELNEC PTE in November 1969.

101	TRJ101		AEC Reliance 2MU3RV		Weyman Fanfare		C26F	1962		

102-110			AEC Reliance 2MU3RV		Weymann		B45F	1962		
102	TRJ102	104	TRJ104	106	TRJ106	108	TRJ108	110	TRJ110	
103	TRJ103	105	TRJ105	107	TRJ107	109	TRJ109			

111-140			Daimler CVG6		Metro-Cammell		H37/28R	1962		
111	TRJ111	117	TRJ117	123	TRJ123	129	TRJ129	135	TRJ135
112	TRJ112	118	TRJ118	124	TRJ124	130	TRJ130	136	TRJ136
113	TRJ113	119	TRJ119	125	TRJ125	131	TRJ131	137	TRJ137
114	TRJ114	120	TRJ120	126	TRJ126	132	TRJ132	138	TRJ138
115	TRJ115	121	TRJ121	127	TRJ127	133	TRJ133	139	TRJ139
116	TRJ116	122	TRJ122	128	TRJ128	134	TRJ134	140	TRJ140

141-146			Daimler CVG6		Metro-Cammell		H36/28F	1962		
141	TRJ141	143	TRJ143	144	TRJ144	145	TRJ145	146	TRJ146
142	TRJ142								

147	TRJ147	Daimler Fleetline CRG6LX	Metro-Cammell	H44/31F	1963
148	TRJ148	Daimler Fleetline CRG6LX	Metro-Cammell	H44/31F	1963
149	TRJ149	Leyland Atlantean PDR1/1	Metro-Cammell	H44/33F	1962
150	TRJ150	Leyland Atlantean PDR1/1	Metro-Cammell	H44/33F	1962

151-188			Leyland Titan PD2/40		Metro-Cammell		H36/28F	1963		
151	WRJ151	159	WRJ159	167	WRJ167	175	WRJ175	182	WRJ182
152	WRJ152	160	WRJ160	168	WRJ168	176	WRJ176	183	WRJ183
153	WRJ153	161	WRJ161	169	WRJ169	177	WRJ177	184	WRJ184
154	WRJ154	162	WRJ162	170	WRJ170	178	WRJ178	185	WRJ185
155	WRJ155	163	WRJ163	171	WRJ171	179	WRJ179	186	WRJ186
156	WRJ156	164	WRJ164	172	WRJ172	180	WRJ180	187	WRJ187
157	WRJ157	165	WRJ165	173	WRJ173	181	WRJ181	188	WRJ188
158	WRJ158	166	WRJ166	174	WRJ174				

While buying ultra-conservative Titans, Salford did weigh up the alternatives with small batches of Fleetlines and Atlanteans with Metro-Cammell bodies. This is Atlantean 210, seen returning from Worsley. Note the crest on the upper deck side panels. Salford buses did not carry exterior advertising. *Roy Marshall*

189	ARJ189B	Daimler CCG6			Metro-Cammell		H36/28F	1964		
190	ARJ190B	Daimler CCG6			Metro-Cammell		H36/28F	1964		

191-205

Leyland Titan PD2/40 — Metro-Cammell — H36/28F — 1964

191	ARJ191B	194	ARJ194B	197	ARJ197B	200	ARJ200B	203	ARJ203B
192	ARJ192B	195	ARJ195B	198	ARJ198B	201	ARJ201B	204	ARJ204B
193	ARJ193B	196	ARJ196B	199	ARJ199B	202	ARJ202B	205	ARJ205B

206	ARJ206B	Daimler Fleetline CRG6LX	Metro-Cammell	H44/33F	1964
207	ARJ207B	Daimler Fleetline CRG6LX	Metro-Cammell	H44/33F	1964
208	ARJ208B	Daimler Fleetline CRG6LX	Metro-Cammell	H44/33F	1964
209	ARJ209B	Leyland Atlantean PDR1/1	Metro-Cammell	H44/33F	1964
210	ARJ210B	Leyland Atlantean PDR1/1	Metro-Cammell	H44/33F	1964
211	ARJ211B	Leyland Atlantean PDR1/1	Metro-Cammell	H44/33F	1964

212-232

Leyland Atlantean PDR1/1 — Metro-Cammell — H43/33F — 1965

212	DBA212C	217	DBA217C	221	DBA221C	225	DBA225C	229	DBA229C
213	DBA213C	218	DBA218C	222	DBA222C	226	DBA226C	230	DBA230C
214	DBA214C	219	DBA219C	223	DBA223C	227	DBA227C	231	DBA231C
215	DBA215C	220	DBA220C	224	DBA224C	228	DBA228C	232	DBA232C
216	DBA216C								

233-257

Leyland Titan PD2/40 — Metro-Cammell — H36/28F — 1966

233	FRJ233D	238	FRJ238D	243	FRJ243D	248	FRJ248D	253	FRJ253D
234	FRJ234D	239	FRJ239D	244	FRJ244D	249	FRJ249D	254	FRJ254D
235	FRJ235D	240	FRJ240D	245	FRJ245D	250	FRJ250D	255	FRJ255D
236	FRJ236D	241	FRJ241D	246	FRJ246D	251	FRJ251D	256	FRJ256D
237	FRJ237D	242	FRJ242D	247	FRJ247D	252	FRJ252D	257	FRJ257D

258-282 — Leyland Titan PD2/40 — Metro-Cammell — H36/28F 1967

258	JRJ258E	263	JRJ263E	268	JRJ268E	273	JRJ273E	278	JRJ278E
259	JRJ259E	264	JRJ264E	269	JRJ269E	274	JRJ274E	279	JRJ279E
260	JRJ260E	265	JRJ265E	270	JRJ270E	275	JRJ275E	280	JRJ280E
261	JRJ261E	266	JRJ266E	271	JRJ271E	276	JRJ276E	281	JRJ281E
262	JRJ262E	267	JRJ267E	272	JRJ272E	277	JRJ277E	282	JRJ282E

283-303 — Leyland Atlantean PDR1/1 — Metro-Cammell — H44/33F 1968

283	MRJ283F	288	MRJ288F	292	MRJ292F	296	MRJ296F	300	MRJ300F
284	MRJ284F	289	MRJ289F	293	MRJ293F	297	MRJ297F	301	MRJ301F
285	MRJ285F	290	MRJ290F	294	MRJ294F	298	MRJ298F	302	MRJ302F
286	MRJ286F	291	MRJ291F	295	MRJ295F	299	MRJ299F	303	MRJ303F
287	MRJ287F								

415-440 — Daimler CVG6 — Metro-Cammell — H30/24R 1950-51

415	CRJ415	420	CRJ420	426	CRJ426	431	CRJ431	436	CRJ436
416	CRJ416	422	CRJ422	427	CRJ427	432	CRJ432	437	CRJ437
417	CRJ417	423	CRJ423	428	CRJ428	433	CRJ433	438	CRJ438
418	CRJ418	424	CRJ424	429	CRJ429	434	CRJ434	439	CRJ439
419	CRJ419	425	CRJ425	430	CRJ430	435	CRJ435	440	CRJ440

456-560 — Daimler CVG6 — Metro-Cammell — H30/24R 1951-52

456	FRJ456	473	FRJ473	510	FRJ510	532	FRJ532	546	FRJ546
457	FRJ457	477	FRJ477	511	FRJ511	533	FRJ533	547	FRJ547
458	FRJ458	478	FRJ478	512	FRJ512	534	FRJ534	548	FRJ548
459	FRJ459	479	FRJ479	513	FRJ513	535	FRJ535	549	FRJ549
460	FRJ460	483	FRJ483	515	FRJ515	536	FRJ536	550	FRJ550
461	FRJ461	484	FRJ484	521	FRJ521	537	FRJ537	551	FRJ551
462	FRJ462	485	FRJ485	522	FRJ522	538	FRJ538	552	FRJ552
463	FRJ463	488	FRJ488	524	FRJ524	539	FRJ539	553	FRJ553
464	FRJ464	498	FRJ498	525	FRJ525	540	FRJ540	554	FRJ554
465	FRJ465	502	FRJ502	526	FRJ526	541	FRJ541	555	FRJ555
466	FRJ466	506	FRJ506	527	FRJ527	542	FRJ542	556	FRJ556
467	FRJ467	507	FRJ507	528	FRJ528	543	FRJ543	558	FRJ558
469	FRJ469	508	FRJ508	529	FRJ529	544	FRJ544	560	FRJ560
470	FRJ470	509	FRJ509	531	FRJ531	545	FRJ545		

Livery: Green and cream

Opposite, top: **Salford built up a substantial fleet of Metro-Cammell-bodied Leyland Titans in the 1960s and standardised on the most conservative model, the PD2/40 with exposed radiator, vacuum brakes and manual gearbox. At least they tried to make the job of changing the destination screens an easy one, with the winding handles being extended down so they could be reached from the ground.** Reg Wilson
Opposite, bottom: **Ten AEC Reliance single-decks were owned by Salford, one coach and nine buses for use on route 5 to Peel Green.** *Bill Potter*

Salford had taken large numbers of Daimler buses at the start of the 1950s with many still in the fleet in 1968. At Victoria bus station, 498 is seen on lay over. *Bill Potter*

SOUTHPORT

Southport Corporation Transport Department, Canning Road, Southport

In 1896 Southport Corporation took over the Southport and Birkdale Tramways Company, expanding its sphere of influence in 1918 with the purchase of the BET-owned Southport Tramways Company. Tramcar operation ceased in 1934.

The Corporation's first bus, in 1924, was a locally-manufactured Vulcan. More followed, including rare Emperor double-deckers in 1931 at which time there were 22 Vulcans in operation making Southport one of the UK's biggest users of the marque. However a pair of Leyland Titans purchased in 1929 were a pointer to the future in Southport as in so many other towns, and Titans were the main type in the fleet thereafter.

Southport's most unusual vehicles were a dozen Bedford QL 4x4 open-top seafront buses which operated along the beach. The last were withdrawn in 1966.

The future: The redrawing of local authority boundaries in 1974 saw Southport's bus operations being taken over by the expanded Merseyside PTE.

10	CRN990	Leyland Tiger PS2/5	Burlingham	OB35F	1950	Ribble 1963
11	CRN992	Leyland Tiger PS2/5	Burlingham	OB35F	1950	Ribble 1963
12	CRN993	Leyland Tiger PS2/5	Burlingham	OB35F	1950	Ribble 1963

20-26		Leyland Titan PD2/12		Weymann Aurora		H32/28R		1952		
20	HFY720	22	HFY722	23	HFY723	24	HFY724	25	HFY725	
21	HFY721									

Southport's fleet was made up primarily of Leyland Titans. New in 1957, 40, was a PD2/20 with Weymann bodywork.
Roy Marshall

In the 1960s Southport reverted to exposed radiators for its Titans, but at the same time switched to forward-entrances, on bodywork by Weymann or Metro-Cammell. The last buses of this type were delivered in 1967. *Reg Wilson*

27-36

	Leyland Titan PD2/20			Weymann Aurora			H35/26R*	1954-56	*27-30 are H32/26R	

27	KFY27	29	KFY29	31	LFY31	33	LFY33	35	LFY35
28	KFY28	30	KFY30	32	LFY32	34	LFY34	36	LFY36

37-41

	Leyland Titan PD2/20		Weymann Aurora		H33/28R	1957

37	MWM37	38	MWM38	39	MWM39	40	MWM40	41	MWM41

43-54

	Leyland Titan PD2/40		Weymann Orion		H37/27F	1961-65

43	UWM43	46	UWM46	49	WFY49	51	CWM151C	53	CWM153C
44	UWM44	47	WFY47	50	WFY50	52	CWM152C	54	CWM154C
45	UWM45	48	WFY48						

55	GFY55E	Leyland Titan PD2/40	Metro-Cammell Orion	H37/27F	1967
56	GFY56E	Leyland Titan PD2/40	Metro-Cammell Orion	H37/27F	1967
57	GFY57E	Leyland Titan PD2/40	Metro-Cammell Orion	H37/27F	1967
58	GFY58E	Leyland Titan PD2/40	Metro-Cammell Orion	H37/27F	1967

59-70

	Leyland Panther PSUR1A/1R		Metro-Cammell		B45D	1968

59	HWM59F	62	HWM62F	65	JWM65F	67	JWM67F	69	JWM69F
60	HWM60F	63	HWM63F	66	JWM66F	68	JWM68F	70	JWM70F
61	HWM61F	64	HWM64F						

84-89

	Leyland Titan PD2/3		Leyland		CO30/26R	1947

84	FFY401	85	FFY402	86	FFY403	87	FFY404	89	FFY406

100-110

	Leyland Titan PD2/3		Leyland		H30/26R	1950

99	GFY399	102	GFY402	105	GFY405	107	GFY407	109	GFY409
100	GFY400	103	GFY403	106	GFY406	108	GFY408	110	GFY410
101	GFY401	104	GFY404						

116	GWM816	Crossley SD42/7T	Crossley	B32F	1951

Livery: Cream and red

S H M D

Stalybridge, Hyde, Mossley & Dukinfield Joint Electricity Board, Tame Street, Stalybridge

The SHMD Board was formed in 1901 and began operating electric tramcars in 1904. Motorbus services started in 1925 with eight Thornycrofts, a make which became the SHMD standard until 1936 and included rare Daring double-deck models from 1933. In 1937 a switch was made to Daimler. Sunbeam trolleybuses were ordered in 1939 to replace the last trams, but the outbreak of war saw the trams surviving until 1945, when they were replaced by motorbuses.

Daimlers were the most common type in the postwar fleet, but there was a brief flirtation with Atkinson in the 1950s and this saw SHMD purchase a unique Atkinson double-decker. Between 1953 and 1956 all new buses were of centre-entrance layout. The first Leylands for SHMD appeared in 1958.

The future: SHMD was absorbed by the SELNEC PTE in November 1969.

1-6 — Leyland Titan PD2/37 — Northern Counties — H36/28F — 1962

1	101UTU	3	103UTU	4	104UTU	5	105UTU	6	101UTU
2	102UTU						

7-12 — Daimler CVG6 — Northern Counties — H36/28F — 1964

7	ATU407B	9	ATU409B	10	ATU410B	11	ATU411B	12	ATU412B
8	ATU408B						

13-37 — Daimler Fleetline CRG6LX — Northern Counties — H43/31F — 1965-66

13	GTU113C	18	GTU118C	23	NMA323D	28	NMA328D	33	NMA333D
14	GTU114C	19	GTU119C	24	NMA324D	29	NMA329D	34	NMA334D
15	GTU115C	20	GTU120C	25	NMA325D	30	NMA330D	35	NMA335D
16	GTU116C	21	GTU121C	26	NMA326D	31	NMA331D	36	NMA336D
17	GTU117C	22	NMA122D	27	NMA327D	32	NMA332D	37	NMA337D

38-47 — Daimler Fleetline CRG6LW — Northen Counties — H41/27D — 1967

38	ELG38F	40	ELG40F	42	ELG42F	44	ELG44F	46	ELG46F
39	ELG39F	41	ELG41F	43	ELG43F	45	ELG45F	47	ELG47F

46-55 — Daimler CVD6 — East Lancashire — H30/26R — 1949

46	LMA746	48	LMA748	50	LMA750	52	LMA752	54	LMA754
47	LMA747	49	LMA749	51	LMA751	53	LMA753	55	LMA755

61-66 — Daimler CVD6 — Northern Counties — H30/28R — 1952

61	OMB161	63	OMB163	64	OMB164	65	OMB165	66	OMB166
62	OMB162						

70	UMA370	Atkinson DD	Northern Counties	H35/25C	1955

Opposite, top: **SHMD briefly showed an interest in centre entrances, and the blank window on the lower deck of this Northern Counties-bodied Daimler CVG6 hides the centrally-positioned staircase. 71 was one of six which were new in 1956. Those that followed in 1957 would revert to rear-entrance layout.** *Reg Wilson*
Opposite, bottom: **Rear-entrance Northern Counties bodywork is fitted to 87, which is seen at the Yew Tree Lane terminus of several Dukinfield services.** *Bill Potter*

The first forward-entrance double-deckers for SHMD were six PD2 Titans in 1962 and re-started the numbering series. They had bodywork by Northern Counties as shown by 1, seen leaving Ashton for Stockport. *Roy Marshall*

71-76

		Daimler CVG6				Northern Counties		H35/25C	1956		
71	VTU71	73	VTU73	74	VTU74	75	VTU75	76	VTU76
72	VTU72								

79-84

		Daimler CVG6				Northern Counties		H33/28R	1957		
79	279ATU	81	281ATU	82	282ATU	83	283ATU	84	284ATU
80	280ATU								

85-92

		Leyland Titan PD2/40				Northern Counties		H36/28R	1958		
85	85ETU	87	87ETU	89	89ETU	91	91ETU	92	92ETU
86	86ETU	88	88ETU	90	90ETU				

96	696GTU	Daimler CSG6	Northern Counties	H36/28R	1959
97	697GTU	Daimler CSG6	Northern Counties	H36/28R	1959
98	698GTU	Leyland Titan PD2/40	Northern Counties	H36/28R	1959
99	699GTU	Leyland Titan PD2/40	Northern Counties	H36/28R	1959
105	PLG967	Daimler G6H	Northern Counties	B34C	1953

106-112

		Atkinson PL746H				Northern Counties		B34C	1954-59		
106	SMA868	108	XLG477	110	993GMA	111	994GMA	112	995GMA
107	SMA868	109	XLG470						

113-118

		Bristol RESL6G				Northern Counties		B43F	1967		
113	WMA113E	115	WMA115E	116	YLG716F	117	YLG717F	118	YLG718F
114	WMA114E								

STOCKPORT

Stockport Corporation Transport, Daw Bank, Stockport

Stockport Corporation operated trams for half a century, from 1901 to 1951 - at which time it was the last tramcar operator in Greater Manchester. Three trolleybuses were operated from 1913 to 1919, when they were replaced by AEC buses. After buying Vulcans in 1923-24, Stockport switched to Leylands in 1926 and here as in so many other north-western fleets, Leyland became the main supplier.

In the early postwar years Stockport supported its local manufacturer, Crossley, adding 65 DD42s to its fleet. It bought Crossley bodywork for its 1958 order and this included the last body built by Crossley, on a Leyland Tiger Cub chassis. Most subsequent buses were bodied by East Lancs.

The future: Stockport Corporation Transport was absorbed by the SELNEC PTE in November 1969.

1-10		Leyland Titan PD2A/30		East Lancashire			H32/28R	1963		
1	YDB1	3	YDB3	5	YDB5	7	YDB7	9	YDB9
2	YDB2	4	YDB4	6	YDB6	8	YDB8	10	YDB10

11-25		Leyland Titan PD2/37		East Lancashire			H36/28R	1964		
11	BJA911B	14	BJA914B	17	BJA917B	20	BJA920B	23	BJA923B
12	BJA912B	15	BJA915B	18	BJA918B	21	BJA921B	24	BJA924B
13	BJA913B	16	BJA916B	19	BJA919B	22	BJA922B	25	BJA925B

26-40		Leyland Titan PD2/40		East Lancashire			H36/28R	1965		
26	FDB326C	29	FDB329C	32	FDB332C	35	FDB335C	38	FDB338C
27	FDB327C	30	FDB330C	33	FDB333C	36	FDB336C	39	FDB339C
28	FDB328C	31	FDB331C	34	FDB334C	37	FDB337C	40	FDB340C

Stockport Corporation ran Titans with all three styles of postwar front end treatment including two batches of PD2A/30s with St Helens-style fronts delivered in 1962-63. They had East Lancs bodies with Stockport's characteristic gutter running above the side windows.
Roy Marshall

131

41-55 — Leyland Titan PD2/40 — East Lancashire — H36/28R — 1966-67

41	HJA941E	44	HJA944E	47	HJA947E	50	HJA950E	53	HJA953E
42	HJA942E	45	HJA945E	48	HJA948E	51	HJA951E	54	HJA954E
43	HJA943E	46	HJA946E	49	HJA949E	52	HJA952E	55	HJA955E

56-70 — Leyland Titan PD2/40 — Neepsend — H36/28R — 1967

56	HJA956E	59	HJA959E	62	HJA962E	65	HJA965E	68	HJA968E
57	HJA957E	60	HJA960E	63	HJA963E	66	HJA966E	69	HJA969E
58	HJA958E	61	HJA961E	64	HJA964E	67	HJA967E	70	HJA970E

71-85 — Leyland Titan PD3/14 — East Lancashire — H38/32R — 1968

71	KJA871F	74	KJA874F	77	KJA877F	80	KJA880F	83	KJA883F
72	KJA872F	75	KJA875F	78	KJA878F	81	KJA881F	84	KJA884F
73	KJA873F	76	KJA876F	79	KJA879F	82	KJA882F	85	KJA885F

265-284 — Leyland Titan PD2/1 — Leyland — H30/26R — 1949

265	DJA173	269	DJA177	273	DJA181	277	DJA185	281	DJA189
266	DJA174	270	DJA178	274	DJA182	278	DJA186	282	DJA190
267	DJA175	271	DJA179	275	DJA183	279	DJA187	283	DJA191
268	DJA176	272	DJA180	276	DJA184	280	DJA188	284	DJA192

285-308 — Leyland Titan PD2/1 — Leyland — H30/26R — 1951

285	EDB539	290	EDB544	295	EDB549	300	EDB554	305	EDB559
286	EDB540	291	EDB545	296	EDB550	301	EDB555	306	EDB560
287	EDB541	292	EDB546	297	EDB551	302	EDB556	307	EDB561
288	EDB542	293	EDB547	298	EDB552	303	EDB557	308	EDB562
289	EDB543	294	EDB548	299	EDB553	304	EDB558		

321-332 — Crossley DD42/7 — Crossley — H30/26R — 1951

321	EDB575	328	EDB582	329	EDB583	330	EDB584	331	EDB585

333-342 — Leyland Titan PD2/30 — Crossley — H33/26R — 1958

333	NDB366	335	NDB368	337	NDB360	339	NDB362	341	NDB364
334	NDB367	336	NDB369	338	NDB361	340	NDB363	342	NDB365

343-352 — Leyland Titan PD2/30 — Longwell Green — H32/28R — 1960

343	PJA913	345	PJA915	347	PJA917	349	PJA919	351	PJA921
344	PJA914	346	PJA916	348	PJA918	350	PJA920	352	PJA922

353-362 — Leyland Titan PD2A/30 — East Lancashire — H32/28R — 1962

353	VDB584	355	VDB586	357	VDB588	359	VDB590	361	VDB592
354	VDB585	356	VDB587	358	VDB589	360	VDB591	362	VDB593

400	NDB353	Leyland Tiger Cub PSUC1/1	Crossley	B44F	1958
401	NDB354	Leyland Tiger Cub PSUC1/1	Crossley	B44F	1958
402	NDB355	Leyland Tiger Cub PSUC1/1	Crossley	B44F	1958
403	NDB356	Leyland Tiger Cub PSUC1/1	Crossley	B44F	1958

404-408 — Leyland Leopard PSU4/1R — East Lancashire — B43D — 1968

404	KDB404F	405	KDB405F	406	KDB406F	407	KDB407F	408	KDB408F

On order: 12 Leyland Titan PD3/East Lancashire.

Livery: Red and white

Opposite, top: **There were few single-deckers in Stockport's fleet. The newest were four East Lancs-bodied Leopards which were delivered in 1968.** *Reg Wilson*
Opposite, bottom: **From 1964 all of Stockport's Titans had traditional exposed radiators, as shown by a 1965 PD2/40 with East Lancs body. Its final Titans would be generally similar, but longer, PD3s.** *Reg Wilson*

WALLASEY

Wallasey Corporation Motors, Seaview Road, Liscard, Wallasey

In March 1901 Wallasey Urban District Council took over the horse tram operations of the Wallasey United Tramway and Omnibus Co. These were electrified in 1903 with a fleet of 30 new 56-seat double-deck trams.

Six AECs introduced municipal bus operation to Wallasey in 1920 - coincidentally the last year the Corporation bought new tramcars. The tramway system was abandoned between 1929 and 1933, the replacement buses being in the main Leyland Titans and Daimler CP6s. Wallasey was unusual in sticking with petrol engines for its buses. Apart from two diesel-powered AEC Regents in 1931 - which clearly didn't impress - and then two Titans in 1937, all of Wallasey's buses were petrol-engined until 1939. The last petrol-engined buses - Leyland Titan TD5s - were withdrawn in 1951.

Like neighbouring Birkenhead, Wallasey tried the side-engined AEC Q, running two from 1934 to 1943.

Wallasey received no buses during World War II, and from 1946 standardised on Leylands - initially Titans and then, from 1958, Atlanteans. The first production Atlantean to enter passenger service was Wallasey's number 1, on 8 December 1958.

Single-deckers played a small part in the Wallasey fleet, although in 1957 it put into service a pair of new PD2 Titans with eight-year-old Burlingham half-cab coach bodies removed from pre-war Titan chassis. These ran between New Brighton and Wallasey Beach. And after buying 30 high-capacity Atlanteans, in 1962 four 31-seat Albion Nimbuses were purchased and used as one-man buses. A second-hand 13-seat Trojan minibus was bought for a service which operated off the main roads in a residential area in 1963 and was replaced by a new Bedford J2 in 1967.

The future: The Wallasey Corporation bus fleet was absorbed by the Merseyside PTE on 1 December 1969.

1-30			Leyland Atlantean PDR1/1		Metro-Cammell		H44/33F	1958-61		
1	FHF451	7	HHF7	13	HHF13	19	HHF19	25	JHF825
2	FHF452	8	HHF8	14	HHF14	20	HHF20	26	JHF826
3	FHF453	9	HHF9	15	HHF15	21	JHF821	27	JHF827
4	FHF454	10	HHF10	16	HHF16	22	JHF822	28	JHF828
5	FHF455	11	HHF11	17	HHF17	23	JHF823	29	JHF829
6	FHF456	12	HHF12	18	HHF18	24	JHF824	30	JHF830
31	LHF31	Albion Nimbus NS3N		Strachans		DP31F	1962		
32	LHF32	Albion Nimbus NS3N		Strachans		DP31F	1962		
33	LHF33	Albion Nimbus NS3N		Strachans		DP31F	1962		
34	LHF34	Albion Nimbus NS3N		Strachans		DP31F	1962		

Metro-Cammell bodywork is fitted to 57, a 1951 PD2 in the Wallasey fleet. *Reg Wilson*

40	AHF836			Leyland Titan PD2/1		Metro-Cammell			H30/26R	1951		
41	AHF837			Leyland Titan PD2/1		Metro-Cammell			H30/26R	1951		
42	AHF838			Leyland Titan PD2/1		Metro-Cammell			H30/26R	1951		
43	EHF392			Leyland Titan PD2/10		Metro-Cammell (1951)			H30/26R	1957		

44-58				Leyland Titan PD2/1		Metro-Cammell			H30/26R	1951		
44	AHF840	47	AHF843	50	AHF846	53	AHF849	56	AHF852			
45	AHF841	48	AHF844	51	AHF847	54	AHF850	57	AHF853			
46	AHF842	49	AHF845	52	AHF848	55	AHF851	58	AHF854			

59-80				Leyland Titan PD2/12		Weymann			H30/26R	1951-52		
59	BHF45	64	BHF50	69	BHF55	73	BHF492	77	BHF496			
60	BHF46	65	BHF51	70	BHF56	74	BHF493	78	BHF497			
61	BHF47	66	BHF52	71	BHF490	75	BHF494	79	BHF498			
62	BHF48	67	BHF53	72	BHF491	76	BHF495	80	BHF499			
63	BHF49	68	BHF54									

99	DHF162E			Bedford J2SZ10		Duple (Midland)			B19F	1967		

Livery: Sea green and cream

WARRINGTON CORPORATION

Warrington Corporation Transport Department, Wilderspool Causeway, Warrington

Warrington started running electric trams in 1902, followed by petrol-electric motorbuses in 1913. Motorbus operation expanded from the mid-1920s, and buses replaced the Corporation's trams between 1931 and 1935. These included some early double-deckers in 1925; indeed until 1966 all but four of the new buses purchased by Warrington were double-deckers. Postwar purchases included 15 Fodens, the last of which entered service in 1956 and marked the end of the Foden PVD6 model.

In 1939 Suburban Motor Services of Penketh was acquired and seven vehicles added to the Warrington fleet, including two modern double-deckers. There was joint operation with Lancashire United Transport, North Western, Crosville and Naylor of Stockton Heath. Warrington took over Naylor's operation in 1964.

The future: The undertaking became Warrington Borough Transport in 1974's reorganisation of local government and in 1986 was constituted as a limited company, still owned by the local authority.

2-10		Leyland Titan PD2/1		Leyland		H30/26R	1949		
2	FED787	4	FED789	8	FED793	9	FED794	10	FED795
3	FED788	5	FED790						

11-17		Leyland Titan PD2/40		East Lancashire		H37/28R	1964-65		
11	AED26B	13	AED28C	15	AED30C	16	AED31B	17	AED32B
12	AED27B	14	AED29B						

Warrington's new-generation buses were Fleetlines with East Lancs bodies. The first, in 1963, featured fairings over the engine bay to give a smooth rear profile. Later deliveries dispensed with this feature but adopted a curved windscreen.
Reg Wilson

18-31 — Daimler Fleetline CRG6LX — East Lancashire — H45/32F — 1963-67

18	5827ED	21	5830ED	24	5833ED	27	BED734C	30	HED857E
19	5828ED	22	5831ED	25	5834ED	28	BED735C	31	HED858E
20	5829ED	23	5832ED	26	5835ED	29	HED856E		

41-52 — Leyland Titan PD2/40 Sp* — East Lancashire — H34/30F — 1965 — *Special - 7'6" wide

41	BED722C	44	BED725C	47	BED728C	49	BED730C	51	BED732C
42	BED723C	45	BED726C	48	BED729C	50	BED731C	52	BED733C
43	BED724C	46	BED727C							

72-81 — Leyland Titan PD2/10 — Leyland — H30/26R — 1950

72	GED582	74	GED584	76	GED586	79	GED589	81	GED591
73	GED583	75	GED585	77	GED587	80	GED590		

82-89 — Leyland Titan PD2/40 — East Lancashire — H37/28R — 1962

82	3167ED	84	3712ED	86	3714ED	88	3716ED	89	3717ED
83	3168ED	85	3713ED	87	3715ED				

90	HED653E	Leyland Panther Cub PSRC1/1	East Lancashire	B41D	1967
91	KED545F	Leyland Panther Cub PSRC1/1	East Lancashire	B41D	1967
92	KED546F	Leyland Panther Cub PSRC1/1	East Lancashire	B41D	1967
93	KED547F	Leyland Panther Cub PSRC1/1	East Lancashire	B41D	1967
94	NED748G	Bristol RELL6L	East Lancashire	B41D	1968
95	NED749G	Bristol RELL6L	East Lancashire	B41D	1968
97	FED584	Guy Arab III 6LW	Guy	B33F	1949
102	MED168	Foden PVD6	Crossley	H30/28R	1954
103	MED169	Foden PVD6	Crossley	H30/28R	1954
104	MED170	Foden PVD6	Crossley	H30/28R	1955
105	MED171	Leyland Titan PD2/22	East Lancashire	H30/28R	1954
106	MED172	Leyland Titan PD2/22	East Lancashire	H30/28R	1954
107	MED173	Leyland Titan PD2/22	East Lancashire	H30/28R	1954

108-112 — Foden PVD6 — East Lancashire — H30/28R — 1956

108	OED213	109	OED214	110	OED215	111	OED216	112	OED217

Livery: Red and white

In the 1960s Warrington bought both front and rear-engined double-deckers. The old order is illustrated by 13, a 1965 Leyland Titan PD2/40, bodied by East Lancs.
Roy Marshall

WIDNES

Widnes Corporation Motor Omnibus Department, Moor Lane, Widnes

Widnes Corporation never operated trams. Bus operation commenced in 1909 with four Commer double-deckers, reputedly the first in the world with enclosed top decks. From 1914 Widnes standardised on Tilling-Stevens chassis, buying both new and used examples until 1930, the last of which survived until 1948. From 1935 most additions to the fleet were Leylands, although interesting second-hand purchases were four STL-class postwar AEC Regents from London Transport in 1955.

One-man-operation was introduced in 1966 using the fleet's two 1952 Royal Tigers. In the same year the fleet's last new double-deckers were delivered.

The future: Widnes Corporation Transport became Halton Borough Transport in 1974's reorganisation of local government, and in 1986 was constituted as a limited company, still owned by the local authority.

1	GTC661	Leyland Titan PD1	Leyland	H30/26R	1946	
2	GTC662	Leyland Titan PD1	Leyland	H30/26R	1946	
5	HTB67	Leyland Titan PD1A	Leyland	H30/26R	1947	

7-15		Leyland Titan PD2/1	Leyland	H30/26R	1948-50	
7	JTD342	9	JTD344	11	KTJ238	13	MTD411	15	MTD413
8	JTD343	10	KTJ237	12	KTJ239	14	MTD412		

16	NTD251	Leyland Titan PD2/12	Leyland	H30/26R	1951
17	NTD252	Leyland Titan PD2/12	Leyland	H30/26R	1951
18	NTD253	Leyland Royal Tiger PSU1/13	Leyland	B42F	1952
19	NTD254	Leyland Royal Tiger PSU1/13	Leyland	B42F	1952
20	NTE580	Leyland Titan PD2/12	Leyland	H30/26R	1952
21	NTE581	Leyland Titan PD2/12	Leyland	H30/26R	1952
26	69BTB	Leyland Titan PD2/12	East Lancashire	H31/28R	1957
27	70BTB	Leyland Titan PD2/12	East Lancashire	H31/28R	1957

28-43		Leyland Titan PD2/40	East Lancashire	H37/28R*	1959-66	*28-31 are H35/28R
28	631GTF	32	237WTD	35	8290TD	38	HTF644B	41	TTE281D
29	632GTF	33	238WTD	36	6981TJ	39	HTF645B	42	TTE282D
30	561RTF	34	8289TD	37	6982TJ	40	HTF646B	43	TTF283D
31	562RTF								

44-48		Leyland Leopard PSU4/1R	East Lancashire	B42D	1967-68	
44	FTB244F	45	FTB245F	46	FTB246F	47	KTB747F	48	KTB748F

60	FTF208	Daimler CWA6	East Lancashire(1954)	H31/28R	1945

Opposite, top: **Warrington's 110, is a Foden PVD6 seen in the depot.** *Bill Potter*
Opposite, bottom: **Most of the buses operated by Widnes Corporation were Leyland Titans with bodywork by Leyland or, as on number 37, East Lancashire.** *Bill Potter*

WIGAN

Wigan Corporation Transport, Melverley Street, Wigan

Wigan Corporation took over the Wigan and District Tramways Co in 1902 and electrified the system. Motorbuses were introduced in 1919, with double-deck operation starting 10 years later, using the ubiquitous Leyland Titan. Between 1929 and 1931 Wigan bought 49 TD1s to replace its tramcars. The last tram operated in March of that year.

Low bridges in the town dictated the use of side-gangway lowbridge double-deckers. It wasn't until 1950 that a change was made to buying highbridge buses.

From 1929 all new buses for Wigan were Leylands, apart from six wartime deliveries. Early postwar Titans had Leyland bodywork, but following the cessation of bodybuilding by Leyland orders were placed with the town's two body manufacturers, Massey Bros and Northern Counties.

Wigan was an early user of forward-entrance double-deckers, standardising on this layout from 1959.

The future: Wigan was incorporated in the new Greater Manchester metropolitan county which came into being in 1974 and as a consequence its municipal bus fleet was absorbed by the newly-created Greater Manchester PTE.

JP8300-JP8329		Leyland Titan PD2/1		Leyland		H30/26R	1950		
151	JP8300	157	JP8306	12	JP8312	84	JP8318	90	JP8324
152	JP8301	158	JP8307	14	JP8313	85	JP8319	91	JP8325
153	JP8302	159	JP8308	19	JP8314	86	JP8320	163	JP8326
154	JP8303	160	JP8309	26	JP8315	87	JP8321	164	JP8327
155	JP8304	161	JP8310	30	JP8316	88	JP8322	165	JP8328
156	JP8305	162	JP8311	32	JP8317	89	JP8323	92	JP8329

18	JP9061	Leyland Royal Tiger PSU1/13	Northern Counties	B43F	1952
80	JP9062	Leyland Royal Tiger PSU1/13	Northern Counties	B43F	1952
81	JP9063	Leyland Royal Tiger PSU1/13	Northern Counties	B43F	1952
82	JP9064	Leyland Royal Tiger PSU1/13	Northern Counties	B43F	1952

AEK501-AEK512		Leyland Titan PD2/12		Leyland		H30/26R*	1953	*8,15,63,94/7/9, H33/28R	
8	AEK501	63	AEK505	94	AEK507	96	AEK509	98	AEK511
15	AEK502	93	AEK506	95	AEK508	97	AEK510	99	AEK512
16	AEK503								

100	AEK513	Leyland Royal Tiger PSU1/13	Northern Counties	B43F	1953
101	AEK514	Leyland Royal Tiger PSU1/13	Northern Counties	B43F	1953
102	AEK515	Leyland Royal Tiger PSU1/13	Northern Counties	B43F	1953
103	AEK516	Leyland Royal Tiger PSU1/13	Northern Counties	B43F	1953
105	BJP364	Leyland Royal Tiger PSU1/13	Northern Counties	B43F	1955

Opposite, top: Wigan, like Salford, eschewed exterior advertising on its buses and instead placed the town crest on the upper deck side panels. This is a Northern Counties-bodied PD3/2, new in 1959 – the year Wigan switched to forward entrances. Note the short bay amidships which allowed Northern Counties to use the same glass sizes in the other bays as were used on its standard 28ft-long body. *Reg Wilson*
Opposite, bottom: From 1966 Wigan's Titans were exposed-radiator PD2/37s with 64-seat forward-entrance bodies. This 1967 example was bodied by Northern Counties. *A Moyes*

The 1968 North West Bus Handbook

Wigan was the home of two bodybuilders, Northern Counties and Massey, and Wigan Corporation patronised both manufacturers. This is Massey's bodywork for the PD3 on one of four identical buses delivered in 1959. *Roy Marshall*

CEK837-CEK841 Leyland Titan PD2/20   Northern Counties   H32/26R   1956

114	CEK837	119	CEK838	123	CEK839	124	CEK840	125	CEK841

2	DEK105	Leyland Titan PD2/20	Massey	H32/26R	1957
4	DEK106	Leyland Titan PD2/20	Massey	H32/26R	1957
6	DEK107	Leyland Titan PD2/20	Massey	H32/26R	1957

DEK108-DEK113 Leyland Titan PD2/20   Northern Counties   H33/28R   1957

108	DEK108	110	DEK110	111	DEK111	112	DEK112	107	DEK113
109	DEK109								

104	DEK534	Leyland Tiger Cub PSUC1/1	Northern Counties	B43F	1957
106	DEK535	Leyland Tiger Cub PSUC1/1	Northern Counties	B43F	1957
7	DJP751	Leyland Titan PD2/30	Massey	H33/28RD	1958
9	DJP752	Leyland Titan PD2/30	Massey	H33/28RD	1958
10	DJP753	Leyland Titan PD2/30	Massey	H33/28RD	1958

DJP755-DJP759 Leyland Titan PD2/30   Northern Counties   H33/28R   1958

115	DJP754	117	DJP756	118	DJP757	126	DJP758	127	DJP759
116	DJP755								

5	EJP501	Leyland Titan PD3/2	Massey	H41/31F	1959
60	EJP502	Leyland Titan PD3/2	Massey	H41/31F	1959
61	EJP503	Leyland Titan PD3/2	Massey	H41/31F	1959
62	EJP504	Leyland Titan PD3/2	Massey	H41/31F	1959

EJP505-EJP510 Leyland Titan PD3/2   Northern Counties   H39/30F   1959

64	EJP505	66	EJP507	67	EJP508	68	EJP509	128	EJP510
65	EJP506								

1	GJP8	Leyland Titan PD3/2	Massey		H41/29F	1960			
137	GJP9	Leyland Titan PD3/2	Massey		H41/29F	1960			
138	GJP10	Leyland Titan PD3/2	Massey		H41/29F	1960			

GJP11-GJP16 Leyland Titan PD3/2 Northern Counties H40/30F 1960

120	GJP11	**122**	GJP13	**129**	GJP14	**134**	GJP15	**135**	GJP16
121	GJP12								

141	GJP17	Leyland Titan PD3/2	Massey	H41/29F	1960
143	GJP18	Leyland Titan PD3/2	Massey	H41/29F	1960
144	GJP19	Leyland Titan PD3/2	Massey	H41/29F	1960
57	HEK705	Leyland Titan PD3A/2	Massey	H41/29F	1961
58	HEK706	Leyland Titan PD3A/2	Massey	H41/29F	1961
59	HEK707	Leyland Titan PD3A/2	Massey	H41/29F	1961
39	HJP1	Leyland Titan PD3A/2	Massey	H41/29F	1961
40	HJP2	Leyland Titan PD3A/2	Massey	H41/29F	1961
42	HJP3	Leyland Titan PD3A/2	Massey	H41/29F	1961
49	HJP4	Leyland Titan PD3A/2	Massey	H41/29F	1961

HJP5-HJP11 Leyland Titan PD3A/2 Northern Counties H40/30F 1961

51	HJP5	**70**	HJP7	**74**	HJP9	**77**	HJP10	**79**	HJP11
54	HJP6	**71**	HJP8						

21	JJP501	Leyland Tiger Cub PSUC1/1	Massey	B43F	1962
35	JJP502	Leyland Titan PD2A/27	Massey	H37/27F	1962
36	JJP503	Leyland Titan PD2A/27	Massey	H37/27F	1962
37	JJP504	Leyland Titan PD2A/27	Massey	H37/27F	1962
145	JJP505	Leyland Titan PD2A/27	Massey	H37/27F	1962
130	JJP506	Leyland Titan PD2A/27	Northern Counties	H36/28F	1962
131	JJP507	Leyland Titan PD2A/27	Northern Counties	H36/28F	1962
132	JJP508	Leyland Titan PD2A/27	Northern Counties	H36/28F	1962
133	JJP509	Leyland Titan PD2A/27	Northern Counties	H36/28F	1962

KEK739-KEK744 Leyland Titan PD2A/27 Massey H37/27F 1963

41	KEK739	**44**	KEK741	**45**	KEK742	**47**	KEK743	**48**	KEK744
43	KEK740								

KEK745-KEK750 Leyland Titan PD2A/27 Northern Counties H37/27F 1963

52	KEK745	**56**	KEK747	**69**	KEK748	**75**	KEK749	**76**	KEK750
55	KEK746								

The nine-vehicle 1962 intake included one single-deck and four Leyland Titans from both Massey and Northern Counties. Shown here is a Massey version.
Harry Hay

143

The Panther Cub was one of Leyland's less successful 1960s models. It had been developed for Manchester Corporation but with its O.400 engine was generally considered to be underpowered. Wigan had two, both with Massey bodywork. *Roy Marshall*

AEK1B-AEK10B		Leyland Titan PD2A/27		Massey		H37/27F	1964		
146	AEK1B	148	AEK3B	150	AEK5B	11	AEK7B	29	AEK9B
147	AEK2B	149	AEK4B	3	AEK6B	24	AEK8B	31	AEK10B

139	DEK2D	Leyland Titan PD2/37	Massey	H37/27F	1966	
140	DEK3D	Leyland Titan PD2/37	Massey	H37/27F	1966	
72	DEK4E	Leyland Titan PD2/37	Northern Counties	H37/27F	1967	
73	DEK5E	Leyland Titan PD2/37	Northern Counties	H37/27F	1967	
78	DEK6E	Leyland Titan PD2/37	Northern Counties	H37/27F	1967	
113	DEK7E	Leyland Titan PD2/37	Northern Counties	H37/27F	1967	
20	DJP468E	Leyland Panther Cub PSRC1/1	Massey	B43D	1967	
22	EEK1F	Leyland Panther Cub PSRC1/1	Massey	B43D	1967	

FEK1F-FEK9F		Leyland Titan PD2/37		Massey		H37/27F	1968		
25	FEK1F	27	FEK3F	32	FEK5F	34	FEK7F	46	FEK9F
26	FEK2F	28	FEK4F	33	FEK6F	38	FEK8F		

166	FJP566G	Leyland Atlantean PDR1A/1	Northern Counties	H44/27D	1968	

Livery: Crimson and white

ISBN 1 897990 65 0

Published by *British Bus Publishing* Ltd © Feb 2000
The Vyne, 16 St Margaret's Drive, Wellington, Telford, TF1 3PH
Facsimile: 01952 222397